LINCOLNSHIRE IN HISTORY

AND

LINCOLNSHIRE WORTHIES.

HARRISON BROTHERS.]

LINCOLN'S HERITAGE FROM THE AGES.—THE CATHEDRAL, 1902. (View from North East.)

[Lincoln

LINCOLNSHIRE IN HISTORY

And Lincolnshire Worthies.

BY

J. MEDCALF.

(Reprinted, with additions, from the "Lincolnshire Poacher"
County Magazine.)

ILLUSTRATED FROM PHOTOGRAPHS, ETC.

LONDON:

WARD, LOCK & CO., LIMITED.

NEW YORK & MELBOURNE.

1903.

PREFACE.

THESE sketches are offered to the Lincolnshire public, not as authentic history, or complete biography, but as a modest and gentle "appetizer" for more solid fare, to those who take an interest in the history and repute of their County.

So far as they go, authorities have been looked up, and alleged facts verified, but should they appear worthy of anything like keen criticism, it may be remembered that they are not the work of a qualified "writer," but are the result of many years' business connection with the Shire, during which a more than passing interest was aroused in its history and the careers of its leading men.

J. M.

CONTENTS.

CHAP.   PAGE

I.—LIFTING THE CURTAIN 9

II.—BOLINGBROKE, KING OF ENGLAND . . 17

III.—"SAXON OR DANE OR NORMAN WE" . . 33

IV.—WAYNFLEET (AN OLD-TIME BISHOP) . . 46

V.—THE GENESIS OF "CHURCH AND STATE" . 58

VI.—A WORRIED ARCHBISHOP (WHITGIFT) . . 74

VII.—THE SHIRE AND THE PLANTAGENETS . . 81

VIII.—THE GREAT LORD BURLEIGH . . . 90

IX.—"BUBBLE, BUBBLE, TOIL AND TROUBLE" . 106

X.—DR. BUSBY ("THE ROD IS MY SIEVE") . 114

XI.—UPS AND DOWNS OF KINGS 127

XII.—SIR ISAAC NEWTON 136

XIII.—THE THREE HENRYS 147

XIV.—JOHN WESLEY ("THE WORLD IS MY
PARISH") 153

XV.—THE GRAFTING OF THE "ROSE OF LANCA-
SHIRE" 170

XVI.—A SOUL'S SHIPWRECK (DR. DODD) . . 184

XVII.—WHAT IT IS TO BE "BLUFF" (HENRY VIII.) 199

XVIII.—SIR JOHN FRANKLIN 208

XIX.—TUDORS AND STUARTS 218

XX.—ALFRED TENNYSON 231

XXI.—UNTO THESE LAST 240

LIST OF ILLUSTRATIONS.

THE CATHEDRAL, 1902 (VIEW FROM NORTH-EAST) . *Front.*

Facing Page

TYPES OF LINCOLNSHIRE WOMEN 13

ENTRY OF BOLINGBROKE INTO LONDON . . . 24

HENRY IV. (*From an Old Picture*) . . . .⎫
                                          ⎬ 17
AFTER FOUR CENTURIES (IN CANTERBURY CATHEDRAL)⎭

TOMB OF HENRY BOLINGBROKE 31

WILLIAM WAYNFLEET, BISHOP OF WINCHESTER . 46

MAGDALEN COLLEGE, OXFORD 51

WAYNFLEET'S TOMB 57

ARCHBISHOP WHITGIFT 74

WILLIAM CECIL, LORD BURLEIGH 90

BURLEIGH HOUSE, NEAR STAMFORD 97

DR. BUSBY 114

BUSBY'S TOMB, WESTMINSTER ABBEY . . . 122

THE HOUSE IN WHICH SIR ISAAC NEWTON WAS BORN 136

NEWTON'S STATUE AT TRINITY COLLEGE, CAMBRIDGE 146

CITY ROAD CHAPEL, LONDON 161

STATUE OF WESLEY 167

WILLIAM DODD, LL.D. 189

LINCOLN CATHEDRAL (SOUTH PORCH) . . . 204

STATUE OF FRANKLIN IN SPILSBY MARKET PLACE . 209

SIR JOHN FRANKLIN 213

GOVERNMENT PAPER FOUND BY THE FRANKLIN
    SEARCH PARTY 217

SOMERSBY RECTORY (*Birthplace of Tennyson*) . . 231

TENNYSON 237

LINCOLNSHIRE IN HISTORY

AND

Lincolnshire Worthies.

CHAPTER I.

LIFTING THE CURTAIN.

GENTLE reader ! We are not about to slay you with the ponderous club of historical narration and bury you under piles of tedious detail. But you will admit that a county that has a John Wesley for its prophet and divine, and a Tennyson for its poet, which has witnessed the exploits of Hereward the Wake, whose roads, such as the Ermin Street, from Stamford northward, were made by the Romans without any steam rollers or " fal lals " of that kind, and were traversed by Agricola and Augustus, and which has had for a bishop one Cardinal Wolsey, not unknown to fame, *may* have had a record worthy of being noticed even in this age of the sceptical and the " nil admirari." We shall not trouble you as to whether man existed in these regions in the Pre-Glacial period or not, with the characteristics of the Paleolithic or the Neolithic periods, the manners and customs of the cave men, lake dwellers, or other grotesque forms of human life, nor dilate upon those portentous animals the rhinoceros, bison, cave bears, and other " small deer " which lived and moved in these lands so many ages ago, and which have given place through the travail of the centuries to the peaceful contemplative cow, the " willing horse " (or, peradventure, the jibbing one), and the harmless, necessary cat.

As the veil of the past lifts like the morning mist from our native fenland, we discern a somewhat gloomy region of forest and morass, peopled by the race which through all vicissitudes of time and conquest has stamped upon the men of these islands the characteristics of stubborn independence and passionate love of liberty, with much else that is linked for ever with the name of Briton. The Celtic race were then predominant, and we catch glimpses of the Iceni, a branch of the greater Cor-Iceni, whose queen, Boadicea, maddened by the lash of the Romans, shrieked and goaded her people in the neighbouring districts (now Norfolk and Suffolk) into war against her conquerors, and reaped a bloody harvest of revenge ere sealing with the poisoned cup her own final overthrow. A Roman writer speaks of her great stature, the fierceness of her appearance, harsh voice, and mass of dark ruddy hair reaching to her hips, but some of this may have been just a little " worked up." Still, a learned writer quotes from Strabo as to another tribe, the Coritavi, inhabiting parts of Lincolnshire, " To show how tall they

were, I saw, myself, some of their young men at
Rome, and they were taller by six inches than anyone else in the city!" What would we not give
now for the *full* story of Caractacus and those bright-
faced boys from the evolving England, who stood
long afterwards in the Market Place at Rome, and
of whom the future pope whispered "Non Angli,
sed Angeli"?

But pages are limited. We must put down these
slides of our little magic lantern and show another,
just glancing however at Caius Decianus, a proctor
or high officer of some sort in our district, specially
effective, it appears, as road maker, bank builder
(for holding up floods, etc.), and military engineer,
and of whom it is recorded that he was a "hard"
man. Grim enough, no doubt, was that old Roman—a
difficult sort of person for a poor savage and not over
scrupulous Briton to get the blind side of.   Still it
seems a little hard that an epithet like that should
have stuck to a poor fellow all these ages!   Caius
had never been to Sunday School and learnt the
wholesome text, "Be sure your sins will find you
out."

We may not unreasonably credit Caius with
making some of the roads round Lincoln City,
which, we are told, were "carried through the
marshes upon piles."

As the Romans, on account of "home troubles,"
withdrew, they left eleven first and second class
fortified places, of which York and St. Albans were

at the top in rank, and of the other nine " Lindum "
was a leading " Colony "—the still existing " New-
port Arch " at Lincoln, which was one of the minor
entrances to the ancient city, placing the visitor
face to face, so to speak, with the stern legionaries
of old Rome, and their doughty and indomitable
commanders.

Enter the Saxons, and behold our county forming
a great part of the kingdom of South Mercia.   More
than six centuries had passed since, in a stable in a
remote eastern villlage, One was born whose " name
should be above every name," and now at last in
this far-off island, " girt by the (not then) inviolate
sea," that name was spreading, and had reached the
wolds and fens, the swamps and the rising towns and
outlying villages of Lincolnshire.   Thousands were
baptised in the river Trent, and although that is not
in our shire, there is little doubt but that many of
the converts were from our districts, for we get a
glimpse of one Blecan, Governor of Lincoln, who
was amongst them.

The learned writer already quoted mentions the
Saxon cemeteries discovered in many parts of the
country, and specifies one at Sleaford, where some
600 graves were found in a space of 3,000 square
yards, the bodies being placed in a doubled up
position, knees bent and hands in front of face, head
towards the West, and face to the North.

Then comes Edwin the Great, King of Northumbria, with a horde of his men, and " collaring "

By Permission of]

TYPES OF LINCOLNSHIRE WOMEN. (From Dr. Beddoe's "Races of Britain")

[J. W ARROWSMITH, Bristol

(excuse the vernacular, it is the sort of thing
kings always *have* done) the whole province of
Lindsey.

We must not send a shudder through our readers
by aping the style and tedious detail of a school
primer.   We cover ourselves, historically, by the
remark that fire and famine, bloodshed and rapine,
feuds of peoples and fury of kings have, for the
observant eye and the reflective brain, seamed and
furrowed the face of our county to an extent not
exceeded in the history of any other section of these
islands.   Practically the brunt of northern invasion
was for long borne by the Eastern Counties, and the
Celts and Romano-British occupants of Lincolnshire were trodden out or driven off to the west and
north, the Anglo-Danish element being markedly
strong in the county, even to the present day.

Prof. Beddoe in his learned work " The Races of
Britain " (1885), says :—" ' Lendum ' (Lincoln) may
have survived the Anglian conquest ; but the modern
population of Lincoln yields no traces of the fact.
They are a fair and (ahem !) handsome people, with
regular features, blue-eyed says Prof. Phillips ; blue
or light hazel I should say ; the latter hue is very
conspicuous at Boston, where the country folk re-
mind me strongly of the peasantry about Antwerp."

And Dr. Beddoe gives a specimen page of existing
types of population, in which the lovely countenance of a typical Lincoln lady and another of a
Lincolnshire belle are conspicuous.   The ladies of

the county will no doubt accept these with becoming diffidence.

" Lincolnshire is notable in Domesday Book for its evident wealth, and large population, including a multitude of ' Sokemen,' also for the number of considerable landholders dating from the Conquest. . . . There is a list of Lincolnshire landholders, time Henry I., which shows that many of these had lost their possessions and gone under Norman lords."

And the Danes ? Ah ! well. Time passes. We are in A.D. 870, and there is a " raid " going on, which is carried out with not quite the gentle courtesy and confused ineffectiveness of Doctor Jameson. The dear Norsemen, heroes of pictures and poems yet to be, and the admired of 19th century boarding-school young ladies, are ravaging from the Humber southward. The famous monastery of Bardney is pillaged and demolished and the monks all massacred. Any system of compromise was not in the line of those gentlemen, and their motto was " thorough." Then comes, apparently for the rescue, the Saxon Count Algar and Morchar, Lord of Brunner. There is a din of battle for two whole days, a rolling to and fro of contending demons, oaths, curses, and the crash of battle-axe into many a foeman's skull, and Algar and Morchar are swept back by the triumphant Danes with such of their men as they can keep together. As an example of the elasticity of the forms of our Church, and their adaptability to all emergencies, there is an old record of an interpolation in the Litany, "From the fury of the Northmen, Good Lord deliver us ! "

Away speed the victors for Croyland Abbey, rich prize, indeed, for enterprising young men, hungry for something more than three acres and a cow. A little touch of pathos comes out of the old chronicle. Some of the younger monks were sent away by their more sturdy brethren, and the latter " went to prayers." Then from the tower of their abbey they looked out upon flaming villages and a devastated country. They gathered in the choir with a last hope for mercy, but the fierce pagans burst in, smashed tombs and monuments, prodded and sounded here and there for hidden treasure, slaughtered the monks to a man, and set the abbey on fire. Having made these satisfactory arrangements for Lincolnshire they bundled off to do the like for Northamptonshire at Peterboro'.

The Saxons learned wisdom, and stood together against the marauding Vikings as the old British race had *not* stood together against themselves, and a certain wise and hardly-trained King of Wessex, Alfred by name, obtained control of Mercia, and so came consolidation and calmer times for our Lincolnshire, though for a time it had been little more than a Danish province. Still, however, the Norsemen worried pretty considerably, and managed to hold Lincoln city for yet another century (A.D. 941).

Our ancient shire was troubled more than enough with " them there furriners," but the result was an amalgam not altogether un-satisfactory :

> " Saxon or Dane or Norman we,
>   Teuton or Celt or whatever we be,"

the men of Lincolnshire, whether in arts or arms, mechanical skill or commercial enterprise, can generally manage to hold their own.

HENRY IV. (From an Old Picture.)

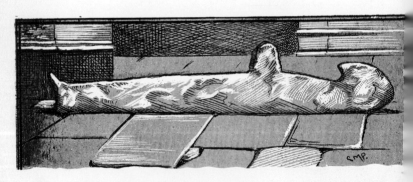

AFTER FOUR CENTURIES, (In Canterbury Cathedral.)

CHAPTER II.

BOLINGBROKE, KING OF ENGLAND.

WE commence these papers with a sketch of
the able and powerful Monarch who first saw
the light in a remote village of our county, and
whose admirers claimed for him the prestige of
being the only King born in this country,
up to their time, in the direct line since the
Conquest. He was born (1367) at Bolingbroke
Castle, the seat of his forbears, originally built by
one William de Romara, about the time of Stephen,
and situated some twenty miles south-east of Lincoln.
After nearly eight centuries there are still distinct
traces of the ancient stronghold, though little but
the foundations. The castle was a spacious square
edifice, with four towers and many apartments,
including a reasonable supply of prison chambers
and warlike means of defence. Surrounded by
hills on three sides, it was open to attack from the
level country only. The Harleian MS. says :—
" If all the roomes in it were repayred and furnished
as it seemes in former tymes they have bin it were
capable to receive a very great Prince with all his

B

trayne." The castle was renovated and extended
by Queen Elizabeth, but in the Civil War it was
surrendered to the Parliament. It was dismantled
and left to decay. As showing the power of Henry's
family, and the folly of Richard II. in entering into
conflict with him, it may be stated that Bolingbroke
was but one of some twenty-one strongholds or
residences, most of them with wide lands adjoining,
at this time in possession of the Gaunt or Lancaster
family. Henry's father was the "old John of
Gaunt" of Shakespeare, fourth son of Edward III.,
his mother the daughter of Henry, Duke of Lancaster. Little seems to be known of Bolingbroke's
boyhood. He was ten years old when Edward III.
died, and he grew up during the weak minority and
early part of the ruinous reign of his cousin, Richard,
son of the Black Prince. An object of suspicion
and of some dread to the reigning King, it was almost
natural that he should pass much of his time abroad,
on the principle, perhaps, of "out of sight, out of
mind." At nineteen, handsome in person, skilled
in arms, and popular with his countrymen, he
married Mary de Bohun, the second richest heiress
in the country (1386). There is little doubt that,
when not on one of his numerous continental trips,
he mostly resided at Bolingbroke, and there are
glimpses in old records of the Duke and Duchess
"giving oblations" at Lincoln, probably in the
Cathedral. Four years after the two cousins were
at a grand "joust" together, near Calais, Henry

showing much bodily strength and address, Richard being not especially noticed. It must have been at this time that the Duke became a member or was otherwise invited to help the order of " Teutonic Knights " in some squabbles in Poland, and with ulterior views against the Turks.

In interesting connection with this we transcribe from current newspapers the following letter of William the Second of Germany (June, 1902) to Edward VII. of Great Britain.

BERLIN, Saturday.

After the re-consecration of the church belonging to the restored Castle of Marienburg on Thursday, the Emperor William sent the following telegram to King Edward :

His Majesty the King, London.

The ceremony of the consecration of the Church of St. Mary, in the Marien- burg, has just taken place, and was most impressive. I beg once more to thank you for your kind letter, which Lord Breadalbane gave me, and for the depu- tation of the Order of St. John which you sent over. It is not the first time that knights tread the soil of the Marien- burg, as tradition here will have it that Earl Henry Bolingbroke (later Henry IV.) came over with an array of English

knights, and fought the heathens side
by side with the knights of the Teutonic
Order, under the guidance of their Grand
Master.

(Signed)   WILHELM I.R.

And our King's reply :

His Imperial Majesty the Emperor
and King, Marienburg, Germany.

Delighted to hear that the consecration of the Church of St. Mary has
passed off so well.   Most grateful for
your kind reception of the deputation
of the Order of St. John of Jerusalem,
sent over after an interval of so
many years.   They are working in
harmony and peace side by side with
the knights of the Teutonic Order.

(Signed)   EDWARD R.

Like most high-spirited young nobles of the
time, Henry wanted to have a go at the " Holy
Sepulchre " business, and in July, 1390, we find
him on the road eastward.   Our trade was then
much mixed with German (or Prussian ?) interests,
many of our Boston houses being held by foreign
merchants.   Henry was stopped somewhere in
Mid-Europe by freebooters and held to heavy
ransom, but this seems to have been looked upon

in the chronicles as a " detail." He was present this same year at the taking of Tunis, and fought against the Norsemen on the Baltic coasts. We may assume that his capture by the robbers must have been a surprise for some small detachment of his party, as he evidently travelled " en grand seigneur," and with strength to resist any ordinary baronial ruffian and his band. An old record states that his " suite included a dozen Knights, a troop of bowmen, six minstrels, a trumpeter, and other musicians, Derby and Lancaster Heralds, and a ' private chapel ! ' " One local writer speaks of " 300 " soldiers, but this is much more likely to have been 150 to 200. Anyhow, it seems to have taken two large vessels to convey this adventurous party, " personally conducted " by Henry, from Boston to Dantzic, when he set forth to Wilna, in Lithuania (now Russia). There they joined their allies in storming a fort, and carried a bridge, the result being greatly due to Henry and his bowmen, and one of the Englishmen being first to plant his flag upon the city walls.

In 1392 the Duke was at Venice, and again essayed for Jerusalem, but again returned unsuccessful, the reason not being clearly shown. It will be seen that the glamour over the east had persistent influence on him through life, and was present with him in his last moments. In 1394 his wife Mary died at twenty-eight, leaving three children, the eldest, Harry of Monmouth, afterwards Henry V.

Two years later he commanded 1,000 English lances at the battle of Nicopolis, against the Turks, in which the Crescent shone, resplendent and alarming, over the Cross. Henry had to run, and with one of the allies, Sigismund, King of Hungary, escaped in a galley down the Danube.

From one of his Eastern journeys he brought back, like any cheap tripper of the 20th century, a lot of curios, no doubt "faked up" for him by the artless paynim or plausible Israelite, but three of them may be held genuine, a parrot, a leopard, and a converted Turk, or "Sarasin," whom he had had, with the thoughtful piety of those days, baptised "Henry."

In 1397 Richard II. accepted the dangerous help of his powerful cousin in overthrowing their uncle, the Duke of Gloucester, and establishing what was supposed to be the final independence and mastership of the King. This, however, proved but the beginning of the end for the "poor Richard" of Monarchs. He thought to get rid of Henry, as he had done of others, by banishment, and on the memorable quarrel between Bolingbroke, now Duke of Hereford, and the Duke of Norfolk, also of the Royal line, he ordered them both across the seas. They went, but Henry was far too strong in family connections, wealth, pledged supporters, and general popularity, to be snuffed out in this way. It was just a case of "au revoir," and no doleful chanting of the "exile's lament." Foolish Richard added

fuel to the fire by declaring the forfeiture of Henry's
estates to the Crown—in plain language, the transfer
of all his cousin's revenues to his own pocket, and
for the more liberal gratification of his own low
tastes. The rest followed in an almost natural
sequence. The country groaned under taxes, "im-
positions," and general misrule. The nobles were
ready for any change ; there was no lineal heir
to Richard, and something had to be done. There
is nothing to show that Henry played the game
unfairly with Richard, nothing to indicate open or
secret disloyalty, until the fat was finally ladled
into the fire by the "confiscation." Then several
leading nobles, with the Archbishop of Canterbury
(already exiled), went over to Henry, laid before
him the deplorable state of the country, and begged
him to accept the crown, and become the saviour
of his people. "This," said the Archbishop, "we
are constrained to offer and intreat. This is both
honourable for you to accept, and easie to be per-
formed, and so much the more, in that no Prince,
by any people have been desired with greater
affection, nor shall be with more duty obeyed."
Henry's reply may savour of double dealing, as has
been often charged, but, on the face of it, it was a
reasoned warning against over-haste, the horrors of
Civil War, and the necessity for full assurance as to
what were the real wishes of the people. "To
cast a King out of state is an enterprise not hastily
to be resolved upon, nor easily affected. . . . Hee

that aimeth at a Kingdom hath no middle course between the life of a Prince and the death of a Traytour," which, at least, shows sound sense and cool judgment. However, he consented, and in 1399 his little expedition landed from three small vessels at Holderness, in Yorkshire, and he and his friends rode forward to London.

He appears to have been received on all hands by acclamation, and, on his part, to have been quite up to the dramatic requirements of the part of the " popular monarch." " Againe the Duke was not negligent to uncover the head, to bow the body, to stretch forth the hand to every meane person, and to use all other complements of popular behaviour. . . . When he came to the citie hee was there likewise very richly and royally entertained, with processions and pageants."

In a speech to his leading councillors he used the remarkable phrase, but quite consistent with our historical precedents : " Alleageance was bound rather to the state of the Realme than the person of the Prince." Ladies and gentlemen of " Divine right " predilections, please note. That thrilling interview between the cousins at Flint Castle followed, when, abandoned by all, friendless and almost homeless, the " King " surrendered to Henry, not even caring to strike one despairing blow for his crown and liberty. An old chronicler describes Richard as " abject and base," Henry as " neither insulting nor relenting, but comforting

ENTRY OF BOLINGBROKE INTO LONDON.

Reproduced by permission of the "Sphere." The original drawing was by the Princess Royal of England (late Empress of Germany).

"With slow, but stately pace, kept on his course,
While all tongues cried—God save thee, Bolingbroke!"

SHAK: RICH. II, ACT 5

and promising friendly, and so the King was brought
to the Tower." Then followed one of the most
dramatic scenes in history—grim indeed in its
association of utter misery with the gaudy trappings
of earthly splendour. The "Kinge was brought
forth, apparelled in his Royall robe; the diademe
on his head, and the Scepter in his hand, and was
placed amongst them in a chaire of estate. . . .
Never Prince so gorgeous with lesse glory and
greater griefe." It might almost be said that
nothing became the sovereignty of Richard like
his leaving it. Amid the tears of many and the
deep emotion of most, he acknowledged that he had
been a bad king, and in a fairly manly and dignified
speech took the blame on himself, and scarcely
sought even to shield himself behind evil associates
and misleading counsellors. He subscribed his
abdication and then "delivered with his owne
hands, the Crowne, the Scepter, and the Robe to
the Duke of Lancaster, wishing unto him more
happiness therewith than had ever happened unto
himselfe." Bolingbroke then claimed the Crown
by right of his Lancastrian blood, though it is true
that, strictly, the young Earl of March stood between
him and that golden evil. He *was* crowned, however, so it is recorded, on the day twelvemonth of
the order for his banishment, so swift had been the
redress of his own wrongs, and so entirely facile
his path to the throne, at the age of thirty-three.

Of Henry's treatment of his unhappy cousin

after his own accession, and that final murder
scene in " Pomfret Castle," there is something to be
said in extenuation. Richard had been a badly
spoilt boy, and he grew into a violent-tempered and
impracticable man. The old chronicles speak of
his beauty of person, love of display, luxurious
living, that he was arbitrary and wilful in the exercise
of power, faithless to his engagements, revengeful.
He is said to have thrashed the Earl of Arundel with
his own hand in Westminster Abbey whilst the
funeral service was going on for his own queen,
just then dead. He spent whole nights in drinking
and debauchery, assisted, one account says, by
two hopeful men of God, the Bishops of Carlisle
and Worcester. When he was parleying with
Bolingbroke, before the surrender at Conway, or
Flint, he remarked to some friends, " Whatever
agreement or peace he (Henry) may make with
me, if I can ever get him into my power, I will
cause him to be foully put to death." No wonder
Henry kept on guard, and took without any
great signs of affliction the news of Richard's
" removal."

Henceforth it is the usual record of English, or,
indeed, of Continental monarchy—conspiracies, open
rebellions, French and Scotch wars, attempts on the
King's life, riotous resistance to taxation, an empty
treasury, and " general distress," seemed, after all,
to more than hint that Henry was not proving the
Heaven-sent ruler of his age. In 1403 he took, for

second wife, Johanna of Brittany, at St. Swithin's minster, Winchester, being married by Henry Beaufort, Bishop of Lincoln, and at that time Chancellor of the Realm. There seems to have been a gleam of sense amid the prevailing chaos in the issue (it is not shown by what authority) of an order that "no lawyer" should be returned as Knight of the Shire to the Parliament of 1404, but this was quickly obliterated by the "House" setting about the confiscation of church property. This, of course, Henry could not stand, as a quarrel with the clergy would probably have been fatal to him. On the contrary, he allowed some sharp measures against heretics, and his reign, in fact, has the unenviable distinction (1401) of being the first in which burning for heresy was adopted, the victim being Chartrys, a clergyman, at Smithfield.

The well-known scene in Shakespeare's Henry IV. (Part I., act iii., scene 1), in which Hotspur, Glendower, and Mortimer, the three conspirators, tumble out as to the division of the kingdom when "Bolingbroke" shall have been disposed of, is piquant and amusing even in these non-Shakespearian days. It is the old story of deciding as to the bear's skin before Bruin has been killed, or, indeed, properly laid hold of. The south and east to Mortimer, west and south-west to Glendower, and *all the north and east* to Percy (Hotspur) ; but there was a curve of the separating river (the Trent, near Gainsboro') which offended the symmetrical eye of Hotspur, who claimed a "rectification of frontiers" by turning the course of the river; and over this he and the fiery Glendower fell to loggerheads. The incident has some historical basis, but the proposed partitioning never came off, owing to unavoidable circumstances, including the utter defeat by Henry of the dealers in bearskin, and the death of gallant Hotspur.

Some ten years of troubled rule succeeded, and then, Harry Bolingbroke, broken in body and mind, an epileptic, suspicious of being supplanted by his own son, and giving way to cruelty and vindictiveness unknown to his younger and brighter days, made ready to lay down his hard won and hard *worn* supremacy.

It is a strange sidelight on the character of this strong statesman, soldier, and monarch that he should have dwelt so persistently on repeating his visits to the east, if not to strike a blow, as formerly, for the " Cross," at least to kneel in prayer before the Holy Sepulchre. Was it some gnawing sense that, after all, he *had* wronged his cousin, *had* usurped a throne to which he had no right, and *had* shed much blood, both patrician and plebeian, in maintaining his power ? Did he shrink from departing " unhousel'd, unaneled, no reckoning made," to that " undiscovered country " where kings and conquerors are but as peasants and chapmen ?   Anyhow, his desire to go on pilgrimage once more must have been keen, for a great council was held at Whitefriars, London, at which the project was dealt with, and Fabyan records : " Large preparations made for the King's pilgrimage to our Lord's tomb at Jerusalem, but even while praying for good speed on his journey, he became so sick that such as were about him feared that he would have died right there, wherefore they, for his comfort, bare him into the Abbot's place (*i.e.*, Westminster Abbey) and lodged him in a chamber, and there, upon a pallet, *laid him before the fire*, where he lay in great agony a certaine of time. At length when he was comen to himself, not knowing where he was, he freyned (enquired) of such as then were about him, what place that was, the which showed to him that it belonged unto the Abbot of West-minster, and for he felt himself so sick, he com-manded to ask if that chamber had any special name, whereunto it was answered that it was named ' Jerusalem.' Then said the King, ' Loving be to the Father of Heaven, for now I know that I shall die in this chamber, according to the prophecy of me before said, that I should die at ' Jerusalem ' ; and so after he made himself ready and died shortly after." So far as we know, he received the last offices of religion from the Abbot, William Colchester, in whose house, of course, the Monarch breathed his last. A strange comment is thrown upon the scene by the suggestion that an oil painting of Richard II. hung in the Jerusalem chamber at the

very time of Henry's death. " Foul deeds will
rise," and this picture may have looked down
with reproachful eyes upon the mortal agony of the
once-triumphant Bolingbroke. It is known there
was such a painting at Westminster, but when
Vertue engraved from it, it was in the Abbey
choir.

Henry's stormy life and hard beset reign was
followed by doubts as to the very disposal of his
poor harmless body. Ostensibly transferred from
Westminster to Canterbury, and there buried with
the usual pomp, it appears that, according to a
MS. in the library of Corpus Christi, Cambridge, a
servant of the King solemnly deposed it was thrown
into the Thames between Barking and Gravesend
during a heavy storm ! The statement was as
solemnly attested by a man of some repute, who
afterwards recorded it as an historical fact. The
conveyance by water may have been convenient
and more expeditious than by road, but sailors
do not like corpses on board, and this servitor
seems to have sworn that in order to allay their
fears and save the vessel, as well as the lives of the
noblemen and gentlemen who were following in
boats, he himself helped to throw the body overboard,
" whereupon there was a great calm." This latter,
however, could not have been greater than the
calm of this wicked story-teller, for the whole of the
gruesome bit of romance has been effectually
disproved. The coffin, with its trappings of cloth

Tomb of Henry Bolingbroke. (Canterbury Cathedral.

From a Photo by]

of gold, etc., got to Canterbury, and was entombed there, the monumental marble over it never having been opened, curiously enough, for four centuries, to test this wonderful tale. But at length, on August 21st, 1832, a part of the tomb was removed in the presence of the Bishop of Oxford, Dean of Canterbury, Sir Charles and Lady Bagot, and officials of the cathedral. Inside a rude wooden case or coffin was found a wrapping of sheet lead, apparently made to fit the body, and on cutting away part of the top front of this, and removing some cloth or linen wrappers, " to the astonishment of all present, the face of the deceased King was seen in complete preservation," the nose elevated, the cartilage even remaining, though, on the admission of the air it sunk rapidly away, and had entirely disappeared before the examination was finished. The skin of the chin was entire, of the consistency and thickness of the " upper leather of a shoe," brown and moist ; the beard thick and matted, and of a deep russet colour. The jaws were perfect, and all the teeth in them, except one fore tooth, which had probably been lost during the King's life.

The general drift of Bolingbroke's career and character, and the incidents of his later days and death, are indicated with sufficient accuracy in the Shakespearian dramas. This sketch has shown the main outlines. He seems to have done his best for his country, to have governed according to the laws, and to have maintained a certain devoutness and purity of personal life not too common with the wearers of the purple. It is no slight addition to such meed of fame as may be awarded to him that his life-history furnished the poet of all time with some of his most striking and enduring lines on that most oppressive and prickly of head gears, a kingly crown.

CHAPTER III.

"Saxon or Dane or Norman, we."

We may well pause in our descent of the stream of history to gaze mentally for a little at that strong, patient, studious, earnest warrior-statesman, the millennial year of whose death it was proposed to commemorate with all honours in 1901. The country had certain special business to attend to in South Africa, however, in that year, and had no particular mind for "celebrations" in other directions —not much stir was made about the great Saxon. Alfred appears to have had little direct connection with Lincolnshire, but it seems pretty clear that he sojourned at the "old hall," at Gainsborough, for a while, on his marriage with Ethelswith, daughter of one of his principal theyns. This was before his accession, and he could only have been just about "of age." It would be an impertinence at this time of day to enlarge on his adventures, or the varied sides of his almost perfect character. But we may note that if he surrendered Lincolnshire, practically, to the Danish power, it was mainly for the purpose of securing his beloved

c

Wessex, in the heart of the island, and with its
southern appendages, as a strong and solid centre
for future operations, and his calm foresight and
steady endurance laid the foundation for that
unification that finally came about. By alternate
hard fighting and wise treaties he bridled the fierce
Northmen, so that from that time the assimilation
of races went on with increasing good will, and Saxon
and Dane, over wide areas of country, learned to
live together. He was the first to perceive that
the wholesale raids by way of the Humber, the
Severn, the Dee, and the Thames, could only be
stopped by "sea power," and he anticipated
Captain Mahan by a small matter of 1,000 years
or so, by placing in the Channel a fleet which grew
under his successor to 100 vessels, with which the
Danes in future had to count, and which, in many
a tough struggle of alternate victory and defeat,
gave trenchant foreshadowing of Aboukir and
Trafalgar. He coded laws, licked society again
and again into shape when stricken to ruin by
furious onslaughts from the North. The memoranda
he left may be taken as the basis for the early
history of our country. He translated the classics,
revived the taste for literature and learning, and
his memorable words have come down to us through
the centuries : " I would that every free-born
youth who possesses means should abide at his
book." With marauding commandoes of Danes
always on the prowl, elementary education, with

the inestimable blessing of a rate at so much in the
£, had not yet become a question of "practical
politics." Yet, withal, this wise, simple, manly,
and pious prince was as hard as nails against the
enemies of his country, marching and counter-
marching, by night or by day, striking a deadly
blow in one place, only to slip away and deliver
a "facer" in some other district. In the Isle of
Athelney, at twenty-nine, with only a scant following, and overborne by numbers, he, though des-
pondent, never really lost heart, and, whether as
the disguised minstrel in the very camp of the
Danes, or as the stern and unyielding leader of an
all but lost cause, amid the shock of armies, he is
revealed to us as the veritable " Kœnig," or " strong
man," of his people. And all this to die at fifty-
two ! We have heard much lately of " grand
old " men—which of them can enter the lists wth
this grand *young* one ? Lincolnshire may feel
proud that he even trod its soil in those early days.

The mighty struggle went on—a great nation
was being born, and the long agony was as of a
" woman in travail." In 921 a great battle was
fought by King Edward the Elder, at Wittering
Heath, just outside Stamford, when the Saxons
won. Edward was recognised as Over Lord of
Mercia and Northumbria—the Welch Kings swore
alliance with him, and the Kings of Scotland and
Strathclyde acknowledged his supremacy. His son,
Athelstane, carried the Saxon dominion to perhaps

its highest point, and " Edgar the Peaceful," with his powerful minister Dunstan, had what some people now-a-days have not, a policy, and that was by judicious and conciliatory measures to forward the welding together of Dane and Saxon. But " the end was not yet." Quarrels and jealousies again broke out, and the sun of the Saxon cause declined from its zenith, and seemed likely to go down in internecine strife. Alfred's great grandson had acted as a sort of coxswain to eight minor Kings, who rowed him down the Dee in that celebrated " eight oar " spin, and the Edwards, the Edgars, and the Athelstanes had bravely played their parts, but weakness and vacillation now came to the throne, and, with the absence of the strong hand, the edifice, so hardly built up, cracked and splintered and tottered to its fall. The Norsemen came on in renewed swarms—there was no united or organised resistance—and the banner of the raven floated victoriously over many a disastrous field.

It was at Gainsborough, about 1002, that the five " boroughs " or " districts," which had been assigned to the Danes by the Saxon Kings (by treaty or conquest), Derby, Leicester, what is now Manchester, and others, and which had been held by them as vassals, formally submitted to Sweyn, who held the port with a powerful fleet, and his armies then ravaged southward, until all England north of the Watling Street came under the Danish yoke. They clove the skull of the Archbishop of

Canterbury with an axe, and the Saxon King Ethelred fled over sea to Normandy. Sweyn's son, the young Canute, was left in charge of the fleet at Gainsborough, while his father went on business journeys to London and other places. Ethelred returned from Normandy and gathered forces for an attempt to recover lost ground, but he could only pillage and destroy. A further struggle was carried on by Edmund Ironside, but it was fated that the Danish flood must for a time submerge the country, and Canute seated himself on the throne of a conquered England. It appears certain that, for at least some time after his accession, he held his court at Gainsborough. He ruled sternly, but with wise caution and much statecraft, as monarch of an all but united nation, and then the strain of Danish fire entered into the veins of the stolid and somewhat easy-going Saxon, and, together with the light-hearted and devil-may-care Celt, went far towards the " making of England." Another strong man was to arise who helped on that process " with a vengeance."

William the Conqueror was an essentially " large-minded " man. He was of the type of warriors who " create a wilderness and call it peace." When he was out of temper he merely butchered a few score of people, burned sundry and miscellaneous towns and villages, and did his best generally to keep down any tendency to over-population. On account of a sneer of the King of France at the

" war-like " Duke of Normandy " lying-in " like a
fanciful body, when he was so ill at Rouen, he arose
from his sick bed and devastated a French province
with fire and slaughter. Even his oaths were
abnormally big. When he wanted to swear badly
he did it by nothing less than the " splendour of
God." His consolidation of this Island Kingdom
by the iron rule, over Saxon and Dane and Celt
alike, as a statesman with a good deal of the brute
in him and no " fine sentiment " whatever, is the
great looming fact of English history, and if he was
not brought personally into such close relations
with Lincolnshire as with other districts of the
country, so much the better for Lincolnshire. But
it was in our county that he met, perhaps, the most
dogged and prolonged resistance to his own fierce
and dominant spirit. " Hereward the Saxon," in
his early love of and practice in all kinds of manly
sports, his gallantry in fight, his resource in a desperate campaign with an overpowering foe, his
unswerving adherence to a practically lost cause
while there was just one faint hope of victory, and
his prudent consent to honourable terms offered
by William when all chance had faded from him,
marks some of the best features of the Saxon
character, and justifies those of us who pride ourselves as Englishmen in classing him fondly as next
only to Alfred and to Harold. He would have
taken high place in our gallery of " Lincolnshire
Worthies," but there appears grave doubt as to

where he was really born, and as we wish that series to include those only of unquestioned birth in the county, we content ourselves with noticing here a few points in the career of this last typical Saxon patriot.

Heraldic research seems to have traced Hereward's blood connection with the Howards of our Mediæval and Modern Dukedom—Ingulf and Matthew Paris are quoted as showing that a Howard or Hereward was well to the front about A.D. 960, in King Edgar's time, and there is not much doubt that *his* son Leofric was the father of our Hereward. On his return, after banishment, the Saxon chief was allowed some of his ancestral possessions, Wigenhall and the Norfolk lands. Then, later, there is a Chief Justice, Sir William Howard, at Wigenhall, and *his* grandson was Admiral and " Captain " of the King's Navy, in Edward III.'s time. One of his girl descendants married " De Mowbray," Duke of Norfolk, and of kin to the Plantagenets, and hence came the long line of Howards and Fitzalans illustrious in English history. A noble lineage indeed !

Professor Freeman acknowledges that " Hereward was assuredly a man of Lincolnshire," and General Harward, who claims kinship with the " Herewards," has gathered some interesting particulars of his boyhood, his leadership in youthful games, his skill in fence, and his contempt for the young Norman nobles then swarming over here, and who savoured more of the fop and the exquisite than the sportsman or the warrior. It was for some horse-play with these, in which Hereward's rude strength was more in evidence than his respect for their dignity, that (in Edward the Confessor's time) the young Saxon was banished, and only heard from afar of the catastrophe of Hastings, the mournful fate of Harold, and the ravaging of his country by the triumphant Normans. He returned and opened communications with some of the yet unsubdued theyns who gathered in and about the Isle of Ely. His claim of ancient lineage, partial royal blood, and as the son of Earl Leofric of Mercia, Lord of Brunne or Bourne, gave him the leadership. The direct race of Alfred had " gone under," and of the great English Earls but one or two were left. Hereward seems to have been at this time about thirty-five years old, of great personal strength and a master of sword, cross-bow, battle-axe, and lance. Just before his more prominent appearance the Saxons and Danes had made common cause, and by the Humber, the Ouse, and the Trent had worried the Conqueror's levies to such purpose that he himself, as saith the Old Saxon Chronicle, " went into those parts and laid them all waste," no doubt swearing as usual.

Hereward commenced a " forward movement " by pillaging and burning Peterboro' Abbey, not an admirable exploit from the " Saxon Hero " point of view, but times were hard and scruples at a serious discount. His tactics were those of Alfred, dodging here and there, striking where least expected, and then scuttling off to some distant and unguarded district, and hitting again, always, for some time, returning to his fortified camp in the Isle to beat off all the furious efforts of William's men to get at him. He plagiarised from the great Alfred's own favourite role by entering the lines of the investing Normans in disguise, and learning the secrets of their forces and dispositions. At one time he appears to have roved the country with something like 4,000 men, and altogether to have so touched up the irate Conqueror by killing some of his best captains, fighting desperate duels, and capturing and holding to ransom rich Norman Abbots, that the " Over Lord " turned from other business to besiege Hereward in person in the Isle of Ely. Even then the tenacious Saxon stood at bay, and with many a rude buffet smote the Norman forces until treachery lent them its aid, and a secret way into Hereward's camp was betrayed to them. Then came a great battle, the weaker was worsted, and the Saxon Earls surrendered, the Old Chronicle adding " excepting only Hereward " and his followers, " whom he led off with great valour."

He made for Bourne, and there, in the woods and marshes adjacent to his family home, renewed the struggle. The woods are still there, very much in many places as he left them, and there, too, are the great yew trees from which, or their progenitors, many a stout bow was fashioned in the brave days of old. As to the marshes, the writer may say that in spite of centuries of improvement, and all the refinements of nineteenth century drainage, he saw only a few years since, looking from near the present Bourne station, a stretch of nine miles under water, with here and there a half-submerged farm house. There need be no question about the main feature of the landscape being water then.

Hereward's mother is said to have been the daughter of Thorold, Sheriff of Lincolnshire, a name not unknown in the county now, and there was no doubt much quiet connivance with the so-called rebel. He would ride forty miles in a night, surprise some Norman stronghold, kill or drive off the garrison, burn the fort, and be back in his woods at Bourne before his foes could muster strength to tackle him in his retreat. He once broke into his own hall appropriated by one of the Norman Nobles, and in the midst of their singing and dancing killed or dispersed them all. "There is nothing new under the sun," and his tactics were just about those of the Boer guerillas of the recent Cape War. At length he made a useful haul. He captured one Ivo de Taillebois (any relation to the Talboys of the present day ?), to whom William had given wide lands in the district. This man seems to have married a daughter of the old Royal House of Mercia. He was " Lord of Spalding and all Holland,"

kept quite a little stately court of his own, and no
doubt held his nose in the air as a very considerable
swell indeed. William was wanting to get the
country settled ; Hereward saw the hopelessness of
any final success ; so they made terms, the Norman
securing his henchman Taillebois in safety as well
as a strong Saxon supporter, and Hereward recover-
ing some of his possessions, with a leading place
in the King's armies to fight for what was now
England.

There is little more of his record. One account
shews him to have been killed after all in some
brawl into which he had been provoked by treacherous Normans. But the more reliable story is
that of his dying peacefully in old age, leaving
descendants by his two marriages, whose posterity
are now amongst us under various forms of the
old name. There are traces that he held a " Knight's
Fee " at Evenlode, in Worcestershire, under the
Bishop there as late as 1086, and long after the
supposed murder. Charles Kingsley's fine novel,
" Hereward the Wake," has been criticised as a
sort of fairy tale, with much more imagination in
it than fact, and no doubt his colours were laid on
rather thickly, but that such a hero did exist, and
that his exploits filled a large space in the records
of his time, must be accepted as historical.

Lincolnshire had its share in the kind attentions
of the Conqueror. He gave away its lands with
his own Royal broadmindedness. Near and about

Boston several of his big men were able to squat with comfort to themselves and "satisfaction to their employer." One Walter D'Eyncourt was of them, and we no doubt have his remote cousins in the Tennyson D'Eyncourts and other families of our day. Around Kirton were immense estates of Edwin, Earl of Mercia, and these were conveyed to William's nephew, the Earl of Brittany. But this was more or less the fate of the whole county. To tighten his grip the King built Lincoln Castle, which has the honour of ranking with Hastings, York, and Nottingham in that respect, to say nothing of the Tower of London. To make clearance for the stronghold 240 houses had to be destroyed, but the town had then grown to be one of the most populous and prosperous in the country, so that we are told by William of Malmsbury it was "a market for all sorts of goods coming by land or water," contained 1,700 mansions, and was held by some 900 burgesses.

The reign of the Conqueror saw the rise of many a stately abbey and cathedral founded by those very queer "Christians," the swashbucklering ecclesiastics who came in his train. Remigius was not exactly one of these, but rather a man who "paid his way," and used the mammon of unrighteousness as a "means of grace" in smoothing his own path to Bishoprics. But *que voulez vous ?* A man had either to fight, plot, or bribe in those days, and the last named was perhaps the easiest course of the three. He became first Bishop of Lincoln, founded our glorious cathedral, and, by that act alone, endowed his country with a " thing of beauty and a joy " for succeeding ages.

To William we owe the massive and enduring " Domesday Book," the thoroughness and detail of which entitle him to pose as the champion Stock-taker in English records. The Saxon Chronicle says, not without a reasonable suspicion of bias : " So very narrowly did he cause the survey to be made that there was not a single hide nor a rood of land, nor, it is shameful to relate that which he thought no shame to do, was there an ox or a cow or a pig passed by." There was no " endowment of research " in those days. William and his satellites endowed themselves, and the " research " after odd cows or pigs in Lincolnshire and else-where was sufficiently keen and penetrating.

CHAPTER IV.

AN OLD TIME BISHOP (WILLIAM OF WAYNFLEET).

IN the midst of the wide stretch of fenland, extend-
ing from Ouse to Humber, in the region of mist
and mud banks, of dreamy pensive sunsets and a
somewhat sad-coloured life, of quiet bucolic prosperity, tempered by ague, and in an obscure
townlet contiguous to a "melancholy ocean," as
Lord Beaconsfield said of Ireland, was born one
who was destined to stand in the Councils of Kings,
to take no mean rank in the long line of illustrious
prelates who have held the ancient see of Winchester, and who, also, as Chancellor of the Realm,
took charge with modest dignity of the Great Seal
of England.   His birthplace was—

> " .   .   .   Seated where the roaring wave,
> Parched with the saltening ardour of the sun,
> Washeth fair Lincoln's shores."

Wainfleet was then and for long years a considerable Port, though now not much more than a single
street, on the site of the Roman "Vainona."   The
exact date of his birth seems unknown, but we can

WILLIAM WAYNFLEET,
BISHOP OF WINCHESTER.

(From an Old Picture.)

From a Photo by]   [W. T. GREEN, *Winchester*

fix it within the first few years of the 15th century. Henry IV. was still wearily wearing the crown and swaying the sceptre he had won from the feeble Second Richard, and through all the foreign wars and home turmoils of Harry of Monmouth (Henry V.), and the long reign (or no reign) of his successor, William of Waynfleet advanced from student to Bishop, and from the simple heritage of a country gentleman to the position of a trusted statesman and keeper of the King's conscience, unbiassed by personal interests or the clamours of faction.

The family name was Patten, and they claim kinship with or descent from the " Patine," who is inscribed with other of the Conqueror's followers on the roll of Battle Abbey. Little appears to be known of his childhood, but he is recorded in the Episcopal Registry, Lincoln, as ordained deacon in 1420, and presbyter in January, 1426. He had probably, through family connection, become known to Cardinal Beaufort, then Bishop of Winchester, and uncle to Henry VI., and so the way into King's palaces may have been made smooth. Beaufort made him master of Winchester School (founded by William of Wykeham), 1429, and afterwards master of the chantrey and hospital of St. Mary Magdalen in that town (1438). The Cardinal must have taken the measure of Waynfleet for this sort of work. From this time on the latter founded schools and benefactions of all kinds, attracted to his own personality many of the great scholars who had graduated in Wykeham's fine foundation, and, so far as we can learn, with pure intent and pious zeal did his utmost to promote the true culture of the people of his own and succeeding generations, always coupled with the condition that religion should permeate and inspire all. In an age of much mental darkness, fierce and stormy passions and political bewilderment, he anticipated the German philosopher who, groping his way into the unseen, cried on his death-bed, " Light, more light ! " For thirty-nine years (1447 to 1486) he held the great Bishopric, and through all his weighty functions was simple, kindly, tolerant, and devout. " But," cries the modern " earnest " Protestant, " for all that he was a Roman Catholic, and took his cues from that dreadful old woman in scarlet who holds such an uncomfortable seat on seven hills at once ! " We shall see. Anyhow, it wasn't very " Roman " to become an early patron of the newly-discovered " printing press," and to work in sympathy with Caxton and his wonderful new-fangled wooden machine at the sign of the " Red Pale, in the Almonry at Westminster."

William had early been brought into contact as scholar and divine with Henry VI., and with that Monarch he continued through life in close friendship and confidence. He baptised the infant heir Edward and confirmed him years after, only to hear of his slaughter by the ruthless Richard and the Yorkists. Henry also made a will, in case he should die first, making Waynfleet executor as to the affairs of Margaret of Anjou, also of the King's mother and other relations. If the Bishop died first, the Monarch ordered masses to be sung for his soul. After eleven years' charge of Winchester School he was preferred as Provost to Eton, then the special project of the King, and the result of his own pregnant suggestions. In 1447 he was made Bishop of Winchester, and appears to have taken the oath disclaiming the Pope's right of infringement on any of the prerogatives of the English Crown. His installation was attended by the King and a crowd of Nobles, Bishops, and functionaries. He held his first ordination at his beloved Eton, and he continued his vigilant supervision of that foundation, its additional buildings, and its growing provisions for the youth of the country. When the Wars of the Roses were over, he nursed Eton, Magdalen College, Oxford, King's College, Cambridge, and his school at Waynfleet with about equal generosity, and he was as busily at work at seventy as he had been at thirty-five! It was as the tried and trusted adviser of the King that he was sent for to a priory at Coventry, where the Monarch then was (just recovered from one of his illnesses), and there, in a great court and surrounded by powerful nobles of both parties, received from Henry VI. the Great Seal as Chancellor of the Realm (1456). His simple devotion to the real interests of the country, loyalty to all that was then held

D

to be good and true, and unaffected piety, had
secured him respect and honour from all. He sat,
however, on a commission (1457) with the Archbishop of Canterbury, the Bishop of Lincoln, and
others, to try the Bishop of Chichester for heresy,
which at that time went by the name of Lollardism.
We always give the thing different names in differing
centuries. The actual disease is a sort of pernicious
exercise of the human faculties upon those deep
subjects which the self-appointed past masters in
theology are alone competent to deal with, but the
curious thing was that, when the martyrs to free
thought and " broad views " themselves got the
upper hand anywhere, they immediately discovered
that their own quondam persecutors were suffering
from this mysterious complaint of difference with
the authorities, and set to work to cure *their* patients
in true orthodox style by prison, rack, or, in very
bad cases, fire. In this instance, the Bishop was
condemned to sit at the feet of the Archbishop
while his pestilent books were burnt before his
face, and, of course, he saw that all his opinions
had been wrong ; fire is always so convincing, but
he was a lucky Bishop, no doubt, in having our
William for one of his judges ! Anyhow, it was
nicer to burn his books than to burn HIM. There
is much to be said for Waynfleet's difficult position
in such times.

In 1473, after twenty-six years of Diocesan work,
he was able to arrange for the laying of the founda-

MAGDALEN COLLEGE, OXFORD. (Founded by Bishop Waynfleet.)

tion stone of the new buildings of Magdalen College, which he had years before promoted from a school or hospital, and which one writer calls the " noblest and richest structure in the learned world. . . . Its majestic tower, seen from the east, with its lofty pinnacles and turrets, is a vision of beauty," and, with its melodious peal of bells, has excited the veneration and enthusiasm of successive genera- tions of students. The Bishop loved the " Mag- nificat," and adopted as his motto, " He that is mighty hath done to me great things," and this is inscribed in Latin in the chapel, where also appears the figure of Waynfleet kneeling in prayer before the Virgin. He lived to see the hall, chapel, cloisters, and library completed ; the main tower being the work of after years. We may well associate with the memory of this man the text, " Blessed are the dead who die in the Lord, for their works do follow them." About this time he extended one of the foundation grammar schools, and himself brought 800 books, a commencing " nest egg " for the library at Magdalen. He got the Episcopal or Papal " legatine " authority over Oxford transferred to the see of Winchester.

Three years after there was a notable scene in St. George's Chapel, Windsor. Edward IV., the pride of the House of York, supposed to be firmly seated on the throne, resolved upon a grand revival of the Order of the Garter, for the " Feast of St. George." That chapel may have since witnessed

many a gorgeous pageant, but few, we may suppose,
to surpass this of 1476. Waynfleet had a certain
architect's and designer's interest in the building,
now hallowed by so many memories, and may well
have felt pride at his ideal of a Royal Fane having
found expression in such beauty and grace of
structure. The stately Edward, with his bold and
somewhat truculent knights, in robes of blue velvet,
each in his own seat or "stall," with his banner
overhead, the voice of the Bishop, now growing
old and worn, reciting his office according to the
Roman ritual, the swelling music, and the faint
odour of the mantling incense, must have made up
a scene hard to match. Then next day Waynfleet
sang "High Mass" in the presence of the Queen
(the afterwards "unfortunate" Elizabeth Wood-
ville), who, like our own late revered Victoria,
and our present beloved Alexandra, wore the
insignia of the Order, her great ladies in attendance, with armoured knights, crested barons, and
belted earls in crowds. It was a day of triumph
for the Yorkists, and the haughty Margaret of
Anjou was then eating her manly heart out in the
Tower of London. Doubtless, William of Waynfleet's thought wandered from that proud scene to
his disconsolate patron and friend, Henry VI. of
Lancaster, dispossessed, discrowned, thought of
with scorn as more fitted for the cloister than the
throne, and now dead and done with. Waynfleet
had often visited his old master with godly comfort

and friendly condolence while confined there by Edward IV. There were, also, no doubt, bitter regrets for the fair Eton that had been despoiled by the conquering faction, by annexing its revenues to those of the new Royal Chapel and plundering some of its effects, after all the labour and devotion the pious King and the blameless Bishop had given to it.

We are tempted to dilate upon the details of the Eton foundation, the minute regulations for the boys laid down by Waynfleet, and the indestructible characteristics of the British schoolboy, as evidenced by the Eton of the 15th century and that of the 20th. We must content ourselves with a reliable record as to one Master William Paston (" Paston Letters "), who wrote his elder brother John that he was badly off for pocket-money, was expecting with impatience the arrival of a parcel of " figgs and raisons " by the " barge from London," and finally acknowledges the receipt of " eightpence," with which to buy a pair of slippers. We also note that Friday was appointed as the official " flogging day " for the school, and *that* shows that our bishop was a careful student of the " Wisdom of Solomon."

In 1480 Edward accompanied Waynfleet to Magdalen College and spent the night there, with a great retinue. He was pleased with all he saw and heard, and promised to send his own young nephews. William laboured incessantly at rules and statutes for the sound working of the college,

broad-minded in general scope, but in much detail
laying down what may or may not be done in
daily life, and all with a distinct bias to the effect
that mere learning without religion is but " stubble
and dross." Foppery in dress, luxury of living,
the carrying of swords, and the " wearing of costly
furs," were forbidden. Card playing, frivolous
amusements, noisy games, and the keeping of dogs,
birds, etc., likely to disturb the austere quiet of a
place of study and thought were taboo'd.

Waynfleet was not, of course, a political or
fighting Bishop. Through all the turbulent years
in which he lived he acted as moderator to parties,
smoother of animosities, soft and persuasive recon-
ciler. He was looked up to by the Lancastrians
as the friend and counsellor of their King, and was
yet, with a certain interval of suspicion, trusted by
the warlike and not very scrupulous Edward. He
was never accused of " time serving " or hypocrisy.
He seems to have posed simply as a Christian Bishop,
doing his best to still the storm of men's passions
and to open the way to a *régime* of peace and
goodwill. Even the truculent Richard III. seems
to have bent to his influence, for almost immediately
on his accession (1484) he visited Magdalen College,
commended the Bishop, gave great largess, " fat
bucks " all round for jovial feasting, and showed
much graciousness to founder and students. No
doubt a little uncertainty as to whether it would be
safe to murder the two little princes, then in the

" Tower," at that time, or better to defer the operation for a while, may have troubled his mind, and
formed a sort of " stake in the flesh " in his career
as a Christian monarch.

Who shall grudge Waynfleet the satisfaction of
having lived to see the crowning of Henry VII.,
after the tragedy of Bosworth Field, and the per-
manent establishment of the Lancaster dynasty,
although from old age he was unable to be present ?
It is interesting to know, however, that he sent to
represent him one " Master Richard Mayew," then
President of Magdalen, and that the sum allowed
to this distinguished person for " expenses " was
15s. 3½d. !

He was bountiful in charity, helped the " bonds-
men " still remaining to their liberty (a sort of
survival of serfdom), and was, in the highest sense,
good—Roman Catholic, of course, as we should say
now, but " one of the best," and to be reverenced
by men of all creeds as in very truth " of the Kingdom of Heaven."   When he died he left two
youths in course of study at Magdalen—one afterwards became the celebrated Dean Colet, founder
of St. Paul's School, London ; the other became
Cardinal Wolsey, who, amongst some few other
notable things, founded Christchurch, Oxford.   A
long and illustrious line of Archbishops and Bishops
have since issued from Magdalen, not to mention
one or two Cardinals.

There is record of a great function some twelve

years after Waynfleet took his Bishopric, and which
seems to show his mediatory influence on the fierce
opposing nobles. A number of them walked side
by side in solemn procession to St. Paul's, headed by
Henry VI. in his royal robes and on foot, apparently
with happy grateful heart for mercies vouchsafed,
as he chanced to be then, and for a very brief
period, the accepted King. The Duke of York,
head of the White Rose party, led Margaret of
Anjou. The young Beaufort, Duke of Somerset,
son of the late Protector, strode along by the side
of his enemy, the Earl of Salisbury, with many
more astonishing partnerships, only too fleeting.
The Bishop must have seen the gathering, and
heard the shouts of the people with joyful hopes
that further bloodshed would be spared, but that
was not to be. Both White and Red Roses were
yet to be incarnadined with the best blood of
the nation.

In the spring of 1486 he felt himself drawing near
his end, and calmly prepared to meet that grisly
phantom who carries the all-sweeping scythe.
He made a will leaving all his lands to the use of
Magdalen and others of his good works ; to the
poor, and for masses for himself and some of the
friends who had gone before. He lingered two
or three months after that, and on the very day
of his death (at over eighty) is said to have given
instructions for restoring some almshouses pillaged
by the Yorkist army. He dealt, also, with other

WAYNFLEET'S TOMB. (In the Chantry, Winchester Cathedral.)

matters of charitable business, and kept his faculties to the last. No details of his actual "passing" are attainable, but the scene would surely be in accord with his peaceful, beneficent life. He was buried with much pomp in Winchester Cathedral. The figure on his monument is reputed a good likeness, and one of his biographers says that the "features are those of no ordinary man. A more beautiful brow, and eyes more full of sweetness and intelligence, can hardly be imagined, something of the fire of enthusiasm is there, but it is all softened and tempered with charity:" no doubt the "charity" which "suffereth long and is kind, envieth not, vaunteth not itself, is not puffed up," the charity which *should* lead by the hand her more popular sisters Faith and Hope, but is yet content to be named last of the three, and, indeed, is so often left "out of the programme" altogether.

CHAPTER V.

The Genesis of " Church and State."

There can be no doubt that when William I. had slaughtered his last batch of victims, burnt his last village, and sworn his last oath, and when his strong soul passed away at Rouen to that heavenly kingdom which, of course, awaited him as a good son of the Church, who had stumped-up any number of " benevolences," and founded a lot of abbeys and rich prelacies, he left his sceptre to one whom the intelligent schoolboy of the present day has no hesitation in labelling as a thorough " wrong 'un," his son Rufus.

His immoralities were atrocious, his exactions from his people cruel, and his dealings with the Church cynically commercial. He does not come much into Lincolnshire history except in relation to one of our Lincoln Bishops, and in transactions not creditable either to the sheep or the shepherd, the monarch or the ecclesiastic.

" Simony was rampant in those days," says Canon Venables of Lincoln in the " Diocesan Histories," and we may add that the dignitaries of the church were more of the stamp of the modern drover, bull-throated, hoarse-voiced, and truculent, than of the tender shepherd leading his flock to pasture on the plains of Palestine. Natheless we must concede that they may have often bullied and fought, and bought and sold their offices, from a conviction that the "end justifies the means," and that it was allowable in those rude days to keep the work of the Church going somehow, and even to "obtain the gift of God with money" if no other means were available for securing the power to combat the rampant evils of the time. The man with the red hair worked up into a complete system of business what had been with others an occasional peccadillo. When ecclesiastical offices were vacant he simply kept them so, and got out of the bother of choosing between candidates by making no appointment, and in the meantime, and sometimes for years, pocketing the pay attached to the place. Whenever there was a specially good "line" in bishoprics going, he would just wait till the highest bidder came along, and then the little transaction would be completed with business-like promptitude.

On one occasion Rufus lay ill, supposed to have been sick nearly unto death. He had refused to make Robert Bloet Bishop of Lincoln, but—

> "The devil fell sick, the devil a saint would be,
>   The devil got well, the devil a saint was he!"

He repented, and the appointment was made. Then Rufus got better, and he repented back again. A dispute was got up as to the jurisdiction of York or Canterbury over "Lindsey," which so worried Bloet that it is gravely stated he paid, or allowed to be paid on his behalf, £5,000 (a much larger sum than the same figures now represent) to square the tiresome little matter, and Rufus' convalescence then became complete.

It is worth noting that we have the first record of a bishop *living* in Lincoln in this reign. The king gave Bloet leave to pierce an archway in the city wall to facilitate access to his house, and we understand this doorway is still to be seen, though partially buried. Since " Blecca the Reeve " had helped Paulinus about A.D. 566 to build the first Christian church in " Lindsey," pious and devoted arms had raised similar temples all over the country, and had led the way to that sort of primacy in number and beauty of churches which many think Lincolnshire to possess. Anyhow, the Bishopric stood forth as one of the most powerful buttresses of the Church, consisting as it did of eight surrounding counties added to its own spacious area.

After that little " accident " in the New Forest by which the royal red-haired ruffian was relegated to " his own place," the Conqueror's youngest son, Henry Beauclerk, succeeded with reasonable facility, owing no doubt to his own idea of enlightened self-interest in seizing Winchester, collaring the royal treasure, and getting himself elected King by the " Witan," who probably found a few tit-bits of the treasure sufficiently convincing. The first English-born king of the new dynasty, however, does not come prominently into connection with our shire, except that it was in his reign that a navigable canal was re-made (or the existing waterway enlarged) from the Witham at Lincoln to the Trent at Torksey, nine miles in length, and now known as the " Foss-dyke." This again opened up to the Ouse and the Humber, and enabled Lincoln to get hold of a large share of the export and import trade of the kingdom.

After Henry's death the City of Lincoln was the scene of stirring events during the struggle between King Stephen and the Empress Matilda, Henry's daughter.

One of the most powerful nobles, Ranulph, Earl of Chester, with his half-brother, Earl of Lincoln, both connected by marriage with Saxon Earls, got possession of the castle by fraud and surprise from the partisans of Stephen, who, too weak to resent this, acquiesced for the time, and so successfully feigned friendship that the two brothers left the castle but weakly guarded. The citizens, like those of London, were friends of Stephen, and sent him word of this. He summoned his barons, filled the city with his troops, and invested the castle. Earl Chester escaped and called for help from Matilda's ally, the Earl of Gloucester, natural son of the Conqueror. With combined forces the two arrived at Lincoln just as, after six weeks' siege, the garrison was on the point of surrendering. The King drew out his forces to meet them, and battle must have been joined somewhere on the Witham side, as Chester's forces appear to have been obstructed by a flooded ford on approaching the city. The fight went against Stephen. A large proportion of his assailants were levies of nobles and others who, for one reason or other, had been deprived of their lands by the *de facto* King. They were desperate, and fought not only for property and position but for life, as, in case of defeat, the chances of escape to westward and southward were small indeed.

Their charges were so furious that the King's troops broke and fled on both wings, leaving Stephen with a centre weak in numbers but strong in courage, discipline, and veteran knowledge of war. Stephen's position appears to have been much the same as Harold's at Hastings, assaulted at once by horse and foot, but repulsing charge after charge by sheer bull-dog tenacity and pluck. Then Earl Chester dismounted with all his cavalry, and by solid pressure of a phalanx of heavily-armed men bore in upon the King. The latter, like a lion at bay, struck the Earl on the crest of his helmet with such vigour that he fell senseless, and then Stephen laid about him until first his battle-axe and then his sword broke in his hands (probably he had been working some injudicious contracts with the Birmingham of that time), so that a powerful knight seized him by his helmet and claimed him prisoner, and he surrendered eventually to his cousin the

Earl of Gloucester. Stephen's dispositions have been criticised; he failed to charge his enemies in their weakest places, he weakened his position where it should be strongest, and his generalship was poor, but he fought like a Trojan. The thing reads quite like some of our recent Transvaal experiences.

There is a story of a solemn mass in the Minster, before the battle (December 22nd to 25th), at which Stephen was present and sundry portents occurred. The chain holding the pyx with the reserved sacrament broke and the sacred wafer fell to the ground. The candle held by the King, and about to be handed to Bishop Alexander, was broke in two. The two pieces of the candle may represent to modern unappreciative minds two hypotheses, first, that the chain and candle may have been carefully prepared beforehand by some underhand foe of Stephen, and second, that the whole story was an invention after the fact. Anyhow Stephen has the odium of suffering under the ban of the Church.

He was " haled " off to Bristol as a captive, the city conscientiously sacked, and many of the people carefully massacred, after which it might have been expected that everything would go on in a smooth and amicable manner, the parties wishing each other a merry Christmas and a happy new year. It had all happened at that season when " peace on earth and goodwill to men " is (and was) supposed to be specially in evidence, but no doubt the whole thing was a mistake of somebody's, probably the Court Chronologist's.

However, neither Stephen nor the Empress appears to have desired to take extreme measures with each other. Matilda (or Maud) had Stephen in her power, but Stephen's people had turned the tables by making the Earl of Gloucester, her own half-brother, prisoner. A bargain was come to; the King retained the crown for his life on condition of recognising the young Henry, Matilda's son, as next heir, and Earl Gloucester was released. One stipulation was that Lincoln Castle was to be held by Stephen, but handed over on his death to Henry's party, and there is one old record of somewhat doubtful exactness, but not altogether discredited, which shows Stephen entering the city in triumph on the surrender of the castle, on horseback, in royal robes and wearing his crown, no doubt a goodly pageant one would like to have seen, standing somewhere by the Stonebow.

The man who succeeded Stephen the interloper (a bold warrior but not much of a ruler or statesman) was of a different stamp. He comes not specially into our county record, but he is interesting in his relation to the shining light of Ecclesiastical Lincolnshire, Hugh of Avalon. We heard much recently of this illustrious personality, and need not therefore risk wearying the reader with repetition. Those days and evenings in Lincoln Cathedral in November, 1900, will live in the memory of many.

A man, "*sans peur et sans reproche*;" a monk, of chaste, simple, and guileless life; a bishop, with a scorn for bribes, and yet so "diligent" in the godly "business" of his diocese as to qualify him to "stand before kings." A strange conjuncture, those two! The Monarch, an uncomfortable blend of the Conqueror, his great-grandfather, and the lighter, more volatile, but withal wily nature of the Angevin breed. The Bishop, after a youth and early man-hood of severest self-discipline, calm, suave, bold and authoritative on occasion, but ever ready with the "sweet reasonableness" which he seems to have learnt from the very Master himself. Henry II. had fought *his* way from boyhood against open foes and covert intrigues, and had established his supremacy over these islands and over vast terri-tories on the Continent by, humanly speaking, his own mailed right arm and his own patient, prudent, skilful policy. He had the radiant head gear of his great-uncle Rufus, and the temper of—a demon. In many things he over-rode all opposition, in others he knew when to bend. His hasty words had proved the death warrant of Becket, but he had been to Canterbury (as somebody in our time would *not* go to Canossa), and he had bared his royal back to the monkish smiters to atone for the murder, and this for the good of his kingdom and the urgently-needed rehabilitation of Henry Plantagenet. The influence of the placid, gentle, but yet forceful Hugh, upon the passionate, war-worn, not ungenerous,

E

and politically-troubled temperament of Henry, is somewhat reminiscent of that of a greater than Hugh over the demoniac amongst the hills of Galilee.

In these sketches we do not pretend to give detailed history—only such main points as may lead interested readers to go further with the study of their own county records. Mr. Froude's graphic account of Hugh in his " Short Studies on Great Subjects " (" a Bishop of the 12th Century ") is most picturesque reading. Here are two, not extracts, but shortened paraphrases :—There had been great need of help for the Cistercian Monastery at Witham, Somerset, which Henry had pledged himself to support, and of which Hugh was then prior. The monks were disappointed, not to say enraged, and sought the King. One Girard poured out his wrath in hot language to the royal delinquent, threatening to give up the priory and leave the country, but the monarch remained apparently unmoved. When for want of breath, or by the exhaustion of any language strong enough for the occasion, there was silence in the chamber, Hugh stood with bent head and a look of distress on his careworn face—Henry eyed him askance, and presently exclaimed, " What are *you* thinking of, good man, are *you* preparing to go away and leave our kingdom ? " and Hugh said gently, " I do not despair of you so far, my Lord. Rather I have great sorrow for the troubles and labours which hinder the care for your soul—you are busy now, but some day, when the Lord helps, we will finish the good work begun." Then this passionate but self-restraining, dominant but generous-minded, fierce and warlike but religiously-sentimental King burst into tears, and embracing the pious and placid prior, cried, "By the salvation of my soul, while you have the breath of life you shall not depart from my kingdom! with you I will hold wise counsel, and with you I will take heed of my soul!" This one oath at least he kept rigidly, although the Prior, and, later on, the Bishop of Lincoln, was no smooth-tongued counsellor, but used to pull him up with some particularly straight talks. He often enough went wrong, but never ceased to look upon Hugh as a great "stand-by."

The celebrated interview with Cœur de Lion is worthy of Shakespearean blank verse. Richard was fighting in Normandy, and sent over for more knights, more supplies, more money. Amongst others the Lincoln Bishopric was laid under contribution. Hugh refused. The King was incensed. Hot dispute arose to the point of the Bishop threatening excommunication against some of Richard's officers who were thinking of carrying out the royal orders to seize and confiscate what was held to be Church property. The King threatened death and —other things. Hugh went on not minding, but at last decided to go and talk to the Lion in his temporary "den" at Roche d'Angeli. He arrived while the King was hearing mass in the church there. The Bishop quietly went forward and made obeisance; the King frowned and looked sternly away. " Kiss me, my Lord King," said Hugh, but the Lion still sulked. Now the " kiss " was the ordinary seal of amity between monarch and high ecclesiastic, and of course meant much. " Kiss me, my Lord," again said Hugh, and caught him by the vest and shook him, much, no doubt, as a mother would shake a moody child. " Thou hast not deserved it," grunted Richard. " I *have* deserved it," replied the Bishop and shook him again ! " *Toujours l'audace*," and the holy audacity won. The kiss was yielded, and, notice the point, that as Hugh calmly went on to the altar and became absorbed in the service the King " watched him curiously," in a brown study, no doubt, as to wherein this peculiar brand of " Lion Heart " differed from his own, and by what occult influences it should so often be able to give points to kings. The dispute was made up, but at a private inter-view afterwards the Bishop spoke solemnly to Richard about his " soul," urging him to " confess," and remarking in a most frank and inconvenient manner upon the immorality of his private life. The King seems to have controlled his emotions (or his temper, which ?) and said subsequently to those about him, " If all bishops were like my Lord of Lincoln, not a prince among us could lift his head against them ! "

Reverting, however, to Henry II. It must have been one of the last occasions (and *not* mentioned by Froude) in which the King and Hugh were face to face, when about 1188, while fighting the French in Maine, Henry—already an old man at fifty-six, tired out by the campaigns and diplomatic worries of a long reign, with the abiding shade of Becket at his elbow, the threatened loss of provinces, the desertion of his *three* sons, and the gloomy consciousness that his life was going down in ruin and defeat—called Archbishop Baldwin and our Bishop Hugh from the throng of courtiers to ride with him, and in bitterness of spirit cried blasphemous things against the Saviour who had *not* helped him to defeat that " camp follower," Philip of France. A worse outbreak occurred at Le Mans, his native city, when he had to abandon it to the French; but there is no record that Hugh was with him, and we may conclude that if the Saint of Avalon and of Lincoln could have been constantly at his side the first Plantagenet might have posed better, both as man and monarch.

Another not very well known incident is that of the tomb of " Fair Rosamond." The frail beauty had died and been buried at Godstone Nunnery, and rich gifts had been sent by Henry and her own friends to decorate her last resting-place. A few years later Hugh of Lincoln came along south and found her shrine before the high altar bedight with silk hangings and golden and other " gauds." He

had them swept away till nothing remained but a
stone with the words "Tumba Rosamundæ"
graven upon it. We do not hear what the King
knew of this, but what he *might* have known was
that Hugh was not exactly the person to condone
adultery, or to be a quiet and unmoved witness to
its glorification and embellishment after death. He
would not be likely to excuse the King on account of
his wife being much older than himself, and something of a termagant.

It was in Henry II.'s reign that Lincoln (with
seven or eight other towns) obtained its charter,
the leading position of the city having been already
accentuated by the fact that Henry was crowned
there, or at the adjacent Wickford (1158), in addition
to the orthodox and probably grander ceremony
at Winchester or Westminster.

In the matter of crowning, Henry evidently liked
to "mak' siccar." It is supposed that he did not
actually wear his crown in the City of Lincoln on
account of an old superstition that such an act on
the part of the reigning monarch presaged disaster
of some sort. This King "governed" as well as
"reigned," In his time the Witham was partly
canalised, and thirty miles of embankment built
up. The royal energy and determination quickened
the entire life of the nation. He had taken over at
twenty-one the sovereignty of England, the better
part of Scotland, Wales, and Ireland, as well as the
Norman and Angevin inheritance of about half

modern France—of his thirty-five years' reign, twenty-one were spent in his French possessions, and only about fourteen in this country. But what years!

Henry posted over the whole country, sat for the administration of justice, heard appeals against unjust judges, sent corrupt and oppressive officials to the rightabout, snubbed unruly barons, and, if necessary, fought them, galvanised the sleepy local life of each district, started improvements one year and came back the next to see that they were still " on the go," and at intervals gathered his men about him and marched off to Scotland or Wales to battle for his crown, or directed an expedition against the nobles and kerns of Ireland. Wars and rumours of wars, plot and counter-plot, rebellion of sons, even down to the youngest and favourite one (John), treachery of his Queen ; the deep abiding animosity of foreign foes, and the implacable purpose of the Papacy to over-ride all, such were the influences that beset Henry throughout his life task of consolidating and strengthening his well-loved England—not a perfect character by any means, but, on the whole, one of the pluckiest and most hard-working and common-sense ruling monarchs that ever sat on a throne.

He died at Chinon in the summer of 1189, of, so it is recorded, a " broken heart." His friend and counsellor Hugh lived on to guide and control Richard and John so far as they would have him.

Then he too went his way into the great unknown, not like his master, bitter of spirit, a beaten and disappointed man, with imprecations on his dying lips, but, as he had lived, pure, kindly, and strong with the faith that can remove mountains still burning steadily in his bosom, and the cool, cautious brain doing its work to the last for his Church and his adopted country.   On his road home from one of his Continental Missions he broke down in London (1200), and lay at the " Old Temple " there.   He seems to have known he was " struck," and as for death, he held, quaintly enough, that " we should be worse off if we were not allowed to die at all." He stuck to his hair shirt and much of his ascetic habit, but took cheerily and gratefully all that could be done for him by devoted friends.   High folks came to see him, Archbishop Hubert for one, King John himself for another.   The former he had a little very frank conversation with, and he didn't come again ;   the latter, wily, slippery, and utterly self-seeking,   even   the   patient   Hugh   could   not " away with," and he was received very coolly. When the time came he had a cross of ashes formed on the floor of his room, and gave instructions that at the moment of departure he should be lifted from his bed and placed upon it.   The choristers of St. Paul's had been sent for to chant the " compline " to him for the last time (the late evening service for protection during the night), and, when part of the way through he gave the signal, they laid him on the cross of ashes, and as the singers began the " Nunc Dimittis " he " fell on sleep." Truly a beautiful ending to a beautiful and fruitful life.

They carried him to Lincoln with all but royal honours. Through Hertford, Biggleswade, Bugden, Stamford, and Ancaster the mournful procession wended its solemn way, everywhere met and often accompanied over the late autumn landscape by crowds of old and young, rich and poor, learned and illiterate, high rank and pious penury, all knowing something of the life and work of the good Bishop, and all contributing a sigh, a tear, or a subdued " Amen." On a hill a mile outside Lincoln the cortége was awaited by John himself and King William of Scotland, three archbishops, fourteen bishops, one hundred abbots, and earls and barons as numerous. The King of England and the archbishops took the bier upon their shoulders and bore it " knee deep in mud," it is said, into the cathedral, William of Scotland standing by in tears. In that sacred fane, with solemn dirge and high ceremonial, they left his mortal part, and so passed Hugh of Avalon, sixth Bishop of Lincoln.

CHAPTER VI.

A WORRIED ARCHBISHOP (WHITGIFT).

THE name of John Whitgift has not come down to us as a monumental one. His personality does not gleam from the dark firmament of the past as a star of the first magnitude, as that of a Lanfranc, a Becket, or a Wolsey, but he filled with learning, dignity, and a fair amount of statecraft, the Chair of Primate of all England in confused and troublous times, and he comes rightfully into our little gallery of those who have carried the grit of Lincolnshire into the high places of the earth.

Born at Grimsby in 1530, he passed his prime in the " spacious times of great Elizabeth," was with that shrewish, masterful, and somewhat volatile virgin, in the last gruesome scene, and placed upon the head of James Stuart the Crown of the Three Kingdoms. He witnessed the rise of Shakespeare and of Spenser, of Raleigh and Sir Philip Sydney ; he was contemporary with Bacon, and was deep in Church controversies and the squabbles of factions while Drake was " singeing the beard of the Don " in the Spanish Main and elsewhere.

His father was a decent merchant of the then

Reverendissimus in Christo Pater D.D.
IOHANNES WHITGIFT Archiepiscopus Cantuariensis

(From an Old Picture.)

rising little seaport of Grimsby, and the boy would probably have " blushed unseen " in the counting house, or more openly on the quay or in the market-place, but that he happened to have an uncle who was Abbot of a neighbouring Monastery. The lad's parts had been noticed, his studious habits appreciated, in a sympathetic quarter, and no great persuasion was perhaps necessary to induce the father to extend his education by sending him to a school in London (St. Anthony's), one of the pupils of which had already been Thomas More, afterwards Chancellor and Martyr. At Cambridge he had for tutor John Bradford, one of the most prudent and consistent of the Reformers, and obtained the friend-ship and patronage of Nicolas Ridley, afterwards Bishop of London, to whom he eventually became Chaplain.

The lowering clouds of ecclesiastical strife were gathering on all hands, and, like many another, Whitgift does not seem to have been in a hurry to declare himself openly on either side. He had the reputation of an accomplished scholar, and stood well with regard to court influences, but made no definite pronouncement on the " burning " question of " Protestantism *versus* Popery " until his ordina-tion sermon, when he preached from " I am not ashamed of the Gospel of Christ," and, later on, as Lady Margaret Professor, when he spoke from the words, " *Papa est ille antichristus*." When called to preach before the Queen, he so acquitted himself that that gracious lady was pleased to make a pun, and called the D.D. and prebendary her " white gift." No doubt the courtiers sniggered dutifully at this, on pain of instant execution. Elizabeth's jokes were not to be trifled with. She seems to have seriously proposed to make Whitgift Primate at once, by " depriving " the poor old and blind Grindal of that office, but to Whitgift's lasting honour he refused to favour that high-handed proceeding.

Dean of Lincoln in 1573, and Bishop of Worcester in 1576, there seems to have been little obstruction to the steady, upward trend of this accomplished, genial, charitable, and dutiful son of the Church, and it is pleasant to read of the throng of listeners in St. Mary's Church when he preached his farewell sermon at Cambridge, and of the voluntary escort of admirers who accompanied him for the first few miles on the road to his new charge.

The Queen continued to show her confidence in him by leaving to him the nomination of his prebends, although these were really in the gift of the Crown, also the appointment to Justices of the Peace for Worcester and Warwickshires, and finally by the offer of the Chancellorship on the death of Sir Thomas Bromley. This last he declined as inconsistent with Episcopal duties, and for seven years from his installation at Worcester he worked at the " daily toil, the common round," of a heavy diocese, smoothing difficulties, adjusting quarrels, shepherding his clergy, and defending the position of his Church both by word of mouth, and by book and pamphlet. Then, at the age of fifty-three, he attained the primacy on the death of Grindal, and fulfilled what seems to have been the long-cherished wish of the Queen.

For twenty years Whitgift guided the Church as best he could amid the welter of conflicting creeds and plotting factions, which in those days threatened the very existence of Church and Crown alike. To his self-willed and haughty mistress he used very plain language about Church temporalities and the little sequestrations then going on. He occasionally made very pertinent and, we may judge, not very welcome remarks as to Magna Charta and Her Majesty's coronation oath. To the Puritans, who tried to win him over, he was civil but firm. To those of his clergy who were leaning that way he was decided in adherence to rule, ritual, and precedent. On others, still infected with the virus of " Rome," and determined to pull the people back to the arms of the " lady in scarlet," he laid the kindly hand of remonstrance and injunction. The nation was at hand grips with the Papal power. Religious dissensions were but the thin cloak for Spanish intrigue, priestly dominance, treason, revolution. To take any definite, irrevocable action was but to fling a burning brand into the hotch potch of combustibles, and ensure the ruin which seemed to be impending.

Some say the Archbishop was unstable, if not a mere time-server, and Macaulay speaks of him as a " sycophant and oppressor," but we have all heard from one of that great man's intimates that his main and unpleasant characteristic was that he was " always so cock sure," and he didn't always know or take the trouble to find out. It is not for any one to throw a stone who has not himself had to steer State and Church through a similar crisis. No doubt the greatest weakness of Whitgift's life was his tampering with Calvinism, and his signature to a set of thirteen articles in which, amongst other inconsistencies, the Church of England was committed to the doctrine of predestination in its most aggressive form of " reprobation." These had, of course, to be disowned, but we can allow for age and worry having weakened the mental and moral fibre of the old prelate, and for the almost frantic efforts necessary from time to time to conciliate differences and assuage party hate. His expressed opinion that King James in his acts and ordinances was to be looked upon as " inspired " must be viewed with the same proviso.

On the whole, we have the view of a broad-minded, cultured, conscientious, somewhat stately, but perhaps a little too " politic " ecclesiastic, doing his best in a time of dire difficulty and danger. We get a glimpse of him making up a quarrel between two gentlemen at deadly feud, and, after persuasive words, inducing the surrender of their arms by five hundred of the litigants' retainers to his own men. Another time he enters Canterbury with much pomp and pageantry and an escort of a thousand horsemen. Now he is inditing a pamphlet on some recondite point of Church creed or discipline, in reply to a rather formidable controversialist signing himself "Martin Marprelate," and anon he is in the Star Chamber pleading for a remission of the fines on that same writer. He writes a memorial to the Queen in which are the words, "Madam, Religion is the foundation and cement of human societies," and, that being the "sermon," follows it up years after with the "application," telling the haggard old woman, over whom he was praying, that it must be quite understood she, like everybody else, was a "sinner." He, as Primate of the Anglican Church, meets her successor, James, as a Presbyterian and pedant, and, in less than a year, converts him to the view that the Church of England was by no manner of means the "mother of harlots," but a highly respectable and well-to-do person, just then trimming herself up for a long period of rejuvenescence.

We think of him through the far off years pondering in study or library as he wrote those ninety and more books or tracts in strenuous controversy ; we seem to catch the steady tones of his voice, tempered with a little quaver of age, as he prayed over the dying Queen, and sought to speed that stormy soul over its last dark passage, and we see

him about a year later stepping on to his barge at
Fulham for a journey down the river to Whitehall
and a conference with the bishops on Church matters.
With set face and grave but kindly demeanour he
enters upon that short but fateful voyage. It was
raw cold, the bleak February wind whistled along
the water and struck him with a chill, which was
still upon him when, a day or two afterwards, he
again crossed the Thames from the south to go to
court. He was seized with paralysis, carried to an
inner chamber at Whitehall, ready and affectionate
hands tended him, the King himself came and stood
over his bed as he slowly sank to rest. He died
with the cry repeatedly upon his lips, *Pro Ecclesia
Dei*. Not a *great* man you say ? Well, but, good
people, must we not measure greatness by what it
has to encounter as well as by its own inherent
strength ?

CHAPTER VII.

THE SHIRE AND THE PLANTAGENETS.

THERE is little to show special connection between our shire and the reign of the " Lion Hearted," but frequently impecunious, Richard. In the fifth of his reign we find one Gerard de Camville held Lincoln Castle, and had the government of the city and county granted to him. He was dispossessed, however, shortly afterwards, and at a Parliament held at Nottingham (1193), the King seems to have put the " whole thing " up for public sale. The record doesn't say who bought it, or whether there was anything of a " knock out " between the gallant Monarch and his pure-minded and unselfish associates or not. But every excuse must be made for the Plantagenets. They claimed to live on the heroic principle of doing what one likes with one's own, and this realm of England, with all its belongings, including such trifles as Lincoln City and Castle, was of course their " own." They had a sort of hereditary family trouble in the way of financial " shortage," and had to bend their Royal minds in a certain magnificent style to some vulgar

F

means of " raising the wind." Besides, Richard
was a very pious person, and went a good deal into
crusading and getting himself shut up in foreign
prisons, with troubadours loafing around and en-
couraging his melancholy by chanting favourite
melodies under his window with a kind of vamp
accompaniment on the harp. You couldn't tell a
minstrel in those days to " move on " under a county
council bye-law, and Richard had to endure it,
but it no doubt added much to his well-known
irrascibility on his very infrequent visits to the
country he was supposed to be governing. As a
matter of fact, we believe he was not in England
for any complete year in all his reign, and with his
many interests elsewhere there need be little surprise
that he had not much sentiment to spare for such
common-place matters as the welfare of his island-
people, or the ideal worth of picturesque fortresses.
Naturally he died abroad, but not of a natural
death, his kingdom having been " all abroad," in
another sense, for the greater part of his time.

His brother and successor, John, was such a
thorough " skunk " that we feel it, in some sense,
a degradation to Lincolnshire to be mentioned in
the same paragraph with him. Skunk-like, he has
left behind him an odour of meanness, fraud, ferocity,
and pusillanimity which the rolling centuries and
the successive evolvement of great events have
failed since, in any wise, to sweeten. It must be
some comfort to the Shire to remember that he

caught his last fatal illness on her soil, and that her congenial dampness and mephitic fen atmosphere helped to rid the world (and his country) of a crowned scallawag. False to his father and false to his brother, the oppressor, if not the murderer, of his bright young nephew, Arthur of Brittany ; perjured to the Pope, perjured to his Barons, and doubly-dyed with perjury to his suffering people, our only " John " stands out as a portentous and gloomy example of how *not* to be a king. Alternately defying his enemies with truculent assurance, and snivelling at their feet when he had got the worst of it, now posing as the patriot king of a resolved country that would brook no Papal domination, and anon grovelling before the legate and rendering to him his crown, to be received again as from the Pope and as Rome's " liege man," we need not wonder that no English monarch has ever thought of christening his baby heir by that hated name, or that the English people have never hankered after a John II. One has been enough for all history.

He gave our little Grimsby its first mayor and charter, and it was one of the earliest he granted, on a visit in the second year of his reign, but he grabbed " 55 marks and a palfrey " in return for this kingly beneficence. In 1204 he did the same for Boston. Three years previously he had had a great " pow wow " with his notables and the Scotch lords and knights just outside the walls of Lincoln, and had received the homage of David of

Scotland as his suzerain. For he had much of the Angevin skill in arms and diplomacy, and he marched, fought, and countermarched, negotiated, shuffled and lied as a panther might have done, had it a human brain and speech, and an idea that it was a king of beasts. There seems to have been no want of physical courage, but the *moral* fibre was—not there. He might have been a great sovereign, an Edward or a Henry VII., but he tried to rule by an unwholesome mixture of truckling and bluster, he " sold " everybody all round in his over-reaching cunning, and when the catastrophe came he was without a friend in the world.

He had maintained his hold on Scotland, and had again received the homage of the king (this time William) ; he had reduced the Irish to something like order, and had bridled Llewellyn of Wales ; he had battled against Holy Church and the princes of this world, on the Continent and at home, but the pitiful bank in which he had thought to have hoarded his tyrannies and his treacheries now closed its shutters and " stopped payment." It was at Stamford, in the Easter week of 1215, that the threatening clouds gathered to a head in the shape of four great earls, some forty barons, 2,000 knights, and an " immense " army of retainers. They met for the " dispatch of business," meaning chiefly, the great charter and some tangible security for the liberties and future honest government of this country. Without any of what Carlyle calls

"allonging" and "marchonging," "*vive*" this and
"*à bas*" the other, but with stern and steady
determination to "see the thing through," they
set out to meet the King and his forces, which, after
seizing London, they did at Runnymede. He was
very much of the typical rat in a pit with two or
three capable terriers. Not being strong enough
to crush the barons, and in salutary fear that they
might crush *h,im* he "negotiated," and finally
signed "Magna Charta," with the intention, of
course, of throwing the whole thing over at his
earliest possible convenience. It may be noted that
of two extant copies of this great instrument, one
is in the British Museum Library of London, and
the other in the Library of Lincoln Cathedral.

Having gained a little breathing space, and once
more licked the Pope's feet, King John got him to
annul the charter, so that civil war began again, his
holiness duly helping his worthy feudatory by
issuing sundry interdicts and curses of the well-
known fine old Roman flavour. (Mem : the
heads of the too "Universal Church" never seem
to have been able to draw the line neatly between
reasonable zeal for the interests of their own institution and impertinent interference in the affairs of
other people.) Then the barons made *their* mistake
by calling in Lewis the Dauphin, instead of fighting
on till John should submit to the strong right arm
of his own people. Lewis and his Frenchmen seem
to have been at Stamford in the early summer of

1216, after a successful landing in Kent, and, to
the national shame, an assumption of sovereignty
in London itself. The King fought with all the
tenacity of his race, darting hither and thither
wherever he could score a point, and distracting
the attention of the barons and their allies in something like Napoleonic (1814) fashion.

He found himself in Norfolk at the time one
Gilbert de Gaunt, having occupied the City of
Lincoln for the Barons, was besieging the castle,
which was held for the King. Gilbert had been
made Earl of Lincoln by John, and in accord with
the practice of the times took this graceful way
of acknowledging the royal favour. Resolving to
relieve the castle, John took his forces from Lynn
across the Wash to Fosdyke, and there met with
the well-known catastrophe. As in the case of
another slippery tyrant of an earlier date, the wheels
of his transport vehicles " drave heavily " in the
soft and shifting soil, the waters gathered and rose
upon shouting teamsters and swearing troopers ;
treasure was abandoned, including the regalia, with
most of the stores, and even the portable chapel
which he usually carried with him, and without
which, we are to assume, this God-fearing person
could not properly say his morning and evening
prayers.

This combination of Pharaoh and Louis XI., of
Uriah Heep and Bombastes Furioso, dragged himself
and what remained of his men and goods across

country with such haste as he might to Swineshead, and there, in the Cistercian Abbey, " sick and sorry," he sought refuge for the night. As certain stories go he was poisoned, and one old monkish doggrel shows that the good brother who managed this little business " for King and country " was challenged by the not too confiding monarch to himself drink of the prepared cup. This he did, and then went into the monastery garden and expeditiously died. Another story has it that a gorge of fruit from the garden (for preference plums) caused all the mischief. Anyhow, John's stomach must have been stronger than the monk's, or he had so inured it to hardships by the feeding propensities of some of his race, that a little more or less of the " deleterious " made no difference. He was able to get on his horse next morning and ride for Sleaford, and again next day for Newark, but this stage had to be done in a litter. The grisly hand of death was upon him, and the poison, or more likely the fever, was asserting its mastery, and at Newark Castle, on Ocotber 19th, 1216, nature, with eager hand and scarlet face of shame, rang down the curtain upon the sordid drama of his life. The records of these last days are mostly those of monkish annalists, who had a bad habit of writing as fact what they wished or hoped to be true. The story of the poisoning appears to have been based upon some previous ill-will between these particular monks and the King, but there is no tangible evidence to support the legend, and we must remember in all charity that George Washington, the absolute and unchallengeable ideal of truthfulness, was not born till centuries afterwards, and " truthful James " followed even a long way after *him*. As to the dead King, about the last word of his contemporaries, as quoted by Mr. Green, in his " History of the English People," was " Foul as it is, hell itself is defiled by the fouler presence of John." The constructor of this terse and vigorous sentence would in later years have run George Washington very hard.

In Shakespeare's play of " King John " our great poet has just " made the best of a bad job." He puts some fine sentiments and, here and there, grandiloquent speeches into his mouth, but no art of literary handiwork, not even high poetic genius, could dare to " make a silk purse out of a sow's ear " in the case of John. We can *see* the pomp and pageantry of courts, we can *hear* the thunder of cannon and the clash of steel on steel, with a running accompaniment of sobs from Constance over the fate of her loved Arthur, we can follow the dubious twistings of such a mind as Hubert's, the would-be assassin, and we can enjoy the vivid presentment and rasping tongue of the bluff and warlike Falconbridge, but no poetic licence could have made John other than he was, and Englishmen would have resented any sentimental or excusatory version of his career. Immediately after the Bastard had acknowledged

to Hubert that " half my power this night, passing
these flats, are taken by the tide, these Lincoln
Washes have devoured them," comes the last lurid
scene in which with dying gasps John is made to say :

> " Poisoned ! ill fare ! dead—forsook, cast off !
> And none of you will bid the winter come,
> To thrust his icy fingers in my maw,
> Nor let my kingdom's rivers take their course
> Through my burnt bosom ; nor intreat the north
> To make his bleak winds kiss my parched lips
> And comfort me with cold—I do not ask you much,
> I beg cold comfort, and you are so strait
> And so ungrateful you deny me that."

Was Shakespeare thinking of a similar outcry
from the pit and from one Dives of whom the world
has heard ?   Is it possible that the unhappy John
found pardon and absolution after all in the mercy
that never faileth ? and that he may have been
classed with those others of whom Tennyson
writes :—

> "   .   .   We trust that somehow good
>   Will be the final goal of ill,
>   To pangs of Nature, sins of will,
>   Defects of doubt, and taints of blood ;

> " That nothing walks with aimless feet ;
>   That not one life shall be destroyed,
>   Or cast as rubbish to the void,
>   When God hath made the pile complete."

CHAPTER VIII.

THE GREAT LORD BURLEIGH.

IF it wasn't so dull to repeat things already well known, we should seize this opportunity of reminding the reader that history " repeats itself," or shall we say *her*self ?   She is like the lady of our affections who, having ruled the household (not to mention ourselves, an insignificant item) for many years, never fails to tell us in regard to passing events, however startling and disturbing, such as the bursting of the kitchen boiler, or one's daughter running away with the baker's man, " Really, dear, this kind of thing has happened before. I think you *might* have anticipated something of the sort, under the circumstances," the remark being followed by a hasty retreat of the admonished party to the study, and the banging of a distant door.

A Cecil, and lineal descendant of the great Lord of Burleigh, has been for many years the foremost statesman of the country, and filled, until just lately, with both sovereign and people, almost the very place which for forty years of home difficulties and foreign intrigues his ancestor held   against all

WILLIAM CECIL, LORD BURLEIGH. (From an Old Picture.)

comers! And one might suppose our "Markiss" had in his time made a pretty close study of the mind and methods of Queen Elizabeth's right-hand man. In both cases we see deftness in playing off one set of antagonists against another, a wonderful capacity for keeping a still tongue, and, on occasion, blurting out home truths, and a disregard for minor matters, while weighty questions of national safety or well-being are hanging in the balance. But we reserve for the fitting occasion a parallel between the William of the sixteenth century and the Robert Cecil who has been fated to see the dawn of this yet more wondrous twentieth, and to hold at his beck the puissance and in his brain the counsels of this later Britain.

William Cecil has traced his own descent from the Sitsilts of Wales, a family of the Montgomery and Hereford squirearchy dating from the time of William Rufus. The name worked itself out through Sibsil, Cyssil, and soon to Cecil. He was born at Bourne in or about 1520, his grandfather having come to England and settled at Stamford, where he became Alderman, acquired lands, and actually attained to the quaint dignity of "Keeper of the Swans" for the Fen districts. He made friends of the Willoughby d'Eresbys and other great people. His son, as one of the Royal pages, attended Henry VIII. to the Field of the Cloth of Gold, obtained many offices, including Constable of Warwick Castle and Sheriff of Rutland, and capped his luck

by marrying the heiress of William Heckington, of
Bourne, who brought with her the Burleigh estate,
adjoining the Cecil property, in and around
Stamford.

It was in Heckington's house at Bourne that
" our William " first saw the light as heir to many
a fertile acre, and to a name already known in the
high places of the earth. He was sent to school
at Grantham and Stamford, and at fifteen was
entered at St. John's, Cambridge. There is little
record of his boyish days, but it is said that he was
so diligent in study as to hire at college a bellringer
to call him at 4 a.m., and yet worked late at night,
so laying the foundation, not only for much learning,
but for a " humour in the blood," which was more
or less of a trouble to him the rest of his life. With
all his application he took no degree at college, but
entered at Gray's Inn (1541), and in the same year
married Mary Cheke, sister of a poor college chum.
Shortlived happiness ! She died in less than two
years, leaving a son, the future Sir Thomas and
Lord Exeter, but not destined to carry on the work
and fame of his father as in the case of Robert, the
issue of a second marriage.

It was in Henry VIII.'s presence chamber (1542)
that young Cecil engaged in a Church controversy
with some priests, and seems to have answered
them with such vigour and acumen that the dispute
was noised abroad and came to the King's ears.
He sent for the young fellow, and was so pleased

with his wit and knowledge that the father was invited to solicit a place for him, and he was appointed *Custos brevium* to the Court of Common Pleas.

In December, 1545, he married Mildred, one of the four accomplished daughters of Sir Anthony Cooke, which four were to be afterwards reputed under Elizabeth to be the most learned women in England. There was a " new woman " movement even in those days. The spinet, the buttery, and the embroidery frame were no longer to be regarded as the sole and fitting occupation for ladies. They affected Greek, Latin, and the mathematics, and the unhappy Lady Jane Grey (at seventeen) was a notable case in point. Roger Ascham, the great scholar, a fellow collegian of Cecil's and secretary to Edward VI. and afterwards to Elizabeth, in a letter dated 1550, couples Lady Jane and Mildred Cooke together as two English ladies whom he " cannot omit " to mention. He speaks of Cecil as " young " (just thirty), but " mature in wisdom," and " deeply skilled in letters and affairs."

At twenty-eight, after gaining knowledge and experience in various small offices at Court, he had become secretary to Somerset, the Protector, and it is on record that " everything went through him." Utterly different in character and methods from Alexander, Bonaparte, and William Pitt, he yet showed in his own way how a young man could keep all the threads of a wide and complicated

policy within his own fingers at an age when most
men are content to be learning the very A B C of
Statecraft.

In September, 1550 (*ætat* thirty), he was made
Secretary of State under Edward VI., and at this
time is described as " meanly statured," but fairly
well set, upright and hardy, brown hair and beard,
a keen eye, and of " grave carriage." We may
just note that his status as a pluralist is undeniable.
One of his numerous accumulative appointments
was that of Recorder of Boston (1551).

Edward died in 1553, and in 1554 Cecil was sent
by Mary, with Hastings and Paget, to meet the
Pope's Legate, who was coming to claim restitution
of Church properties, and this was only one of
many instances in which wary William deftly
maintained his balance on the political and ecclesiastical tight rope, in face of an occasionally
grumbling, but, on the whole, puzzled and half-
admiring Europe.

In 1555 he sat as Knight of the Shire for Lincoln
(later on sitting for both Lincoln and Northamptonshire), and on the death of Mary, 1558, he was
appointed by Elizabeth Secretary of State, a
position he, of course, had not held under her sister.
From that time Cecil might almost have taken for
his own the words of Louis XIV., " *L'état, c'est moi*."
For, although he worked under a mistress with the
manners of a bargewoman, and frequently the
language of a fish fag, who was always getting on

the rampage, and who never hesitated to throw any minister or official overboard the moment her own august personality was likely to be compromised, it was Cecil's policy that in the long run prevailed, Cecil's advice became on all points the ruling factor, and Cecil's silent, and at times tortuous, methods became the wondering terror of conspirators at home and crafty or insolent foes abroad.

That he and the Queen suited each other there is little doubt. His quiet, persistent tact and discretion were the complement of her rude and rough Tudor temper. His wide and deep knowledge, held back with marvellous patience up to some precise determining moment of crisis, bridled and overmastered her passionate and haughty nature, till " What does Cecil say ? " and " Send for Cecil," became the habit of her life. He is accused of tergiversation, shuffling, meanness, want of principle in posing at one time as a Protestant and at another as a Papist—let us see !

In our " Whitgift " paper we tried to give some faint idea of the state of things under Elizabeth, both as to Church and State, but for some ten or twelve years *prior* to her accession Cecil was working out a critical and somewhat dangerous apprenticeship in Statecraft. Politics did not then consist in a choice between a " seat in the Cabinet," with audience of the sovereign, and a blissful retirement to one's country seat, with its books, its sports, and its pleasant greenery. The " ups and downs "

meant something. Protector Somerset, Protector
Northumberland, and the rest, habitually skated
on the thinnest of ice. Tower Hill was a sort of
dumping ground for heads of all ages, sexes, and
degrees, from the white haired councillor to the
innocent and cultured girl queen of seventeen. A
Spanish King Consort plotted with gloomy persistence for the destruction of the pestilent nation
that had refused to be governed by him or the
Pope. The country swarmed with Jesuit spies
and conspirators. France watched with eager eyes
and threatening mien for the least chance of
taking a hand in the great game.

The Huguenots of that fair land and of the
Netherlands had to be supported, now secretly,
now openly. Henry of Navarre, the supposed
hope of Protestantism, was kept in tow and used as
a lever against the Roman Catholic powers, only
to turn tail at last with his cynical remark, " After
all, Paris is worth a Mass." Mary Queen of Scots,
as descendant of Henry VII. and claimant to the
thrones, " more or less," as Mark Twain would say,
of England, France, and Scotland, was the centre
of intrigues desperate and untiring, and, as we
know, it was her son James who *did* succeed to the
sovereignty of the United Kingdom. War was
covertly carried on abroad without formal declaration or openly expressed quarrel. If buccaneering
expeditions succeeded, and the injured party had
too much business on hand to resent, they were

BURLEIGH HOUSE, NEAR STAMFORD. (Built by Cecil.)

acknowledged, and the plunder shared between captains, counsellors, courtiers, and Sovereign. If they met with disaster they were promptly dis-owned, and left to any fate their conquerors might ordain or their patrons find convenient.

The so-called offence of " Treason " was about as common as petty larceny is now, and men might well grabble with nervous fingers amongst the fastenings of lace collars in dreamy doubt as to whether their heads were still there or not. The murder of sovereigns and statesmen was almost openly plotted. A leading London paper, recently reviewing Major Hume's book on " Treason and Plot," writes that in the State papers of the time there is " a record of scoundrels and scoundrelism to which it would not be easy to find a parallel. Conspiracies come so thick and fast that the reader is lost in conjecture as to who was betraying whom. Contemporary rulers, no less puzzled, got out of their dilemmas by impartially hanging everybody, a drastic but essentially just solution. *Our* players in the game were more than a match for the most subtle brains of Spain or Italy. Lord Burleigh could beat the best of them ! "

The highest certificate to Cecil's proficiency is, perhaps, the recorded opinions of his opponents, and the almost Imperial status and repute of the Realm when he finally rendered up his stewardship. The Spanish ambassador, Feria, defeated in one of his little projects, writes of him as a " pestilent knave." He mildly reported to his master, Philip, that Elizabeth was " a daughter of the devil, and her chief ministers the greatest scoundrels and heretics in the land." Another, Don Quadra, is a trifle more calm: " Cecil is a very great heretic, but he is neither foolish nor false." A third diplomat from the Spanish King, De Spes, tried *his* hand, and wrote: " Cecil is a crafty fox, a mortal enemy to the Catholics and to our King, and it is necessary to watch his designs very closely, because he proceeds with the greatest caution and dissimulation; " and again: " This man manages the bulk of the business, and by means of his vigilance and craftiness, together with his utter unscrupulousness of word and deed, thinks to outwit the ministers of other princes, which, to some extent, he has hitherto succeeded in doing." The misfortune was that " ministers of other princes " were indignantly grieved that anyone but themselves should be so very unfair as to play the game with loaded dice. They finessed, lied, and shuffled; *he* finessed and, there is little doubt, lied, and shuffled also; *they* wove around him and the Queen a network of spies and corruption; *he* bought over their spies with higher bids, and raised the market price of the written proofs of deadly conspiracy; they suborned per-jurers and murderers, but he was always somewhere behind, either with a little more money or the knowledge of some secret of their past, which frightened them out of their wits, and caused them

to fly for their lives. Cecil was the " Brer Rabbit "
of that golden age. Never did a statesman "lay
low and say nuffin" so effectively. Silent, calm,
scheming, bland, courteous, and indefatigable, he
could receive the most astounding disclosures with
impassive countenance, or a smile, as who should
say, " You don't suppose I didn't know all about
it ? " But under the soft " pads " there lurked
some very feline and formidable claws. Now and
then, when the play had gone distinctly in his
favour, he let himself go—out came the claws, and
there was instantly an ugly gash in the self-con-
fidence and diplomatic dignity of his antagonist.
He told some Spaniards that they must not attend
mass. " What, not foreigners ? " said one of them.
" No," said Cecil bluntly, and turning his back
upon them strode to the Queen's room. He stormed
at the Spanish Ambassador about the expulsion
of our own Envoy from Spain till, it is said, he
stopped " for want of breath." The French Ambassador came to him to " protest " against something, and Cecil says he got a " very short answer,"
adding, " He departed with no small misliking, and
I well contented to utter some round speeches."

That he feathered his own nest is undeniable,
but there is little or nothing to show that this was
done in any discreditable way. He was offered
heavy bribes and pensions to work with the enemies
of his country. His name is down in a Spanish list
for " 1,000 crowns," but—did he get it ? Through-

out his long career there is the clearest evidence
that the one aim he kept in view, and battled for,
was the strength and glory of England, and her
freedom from Papal or any other foreign domination.
As he grew in power, and in the respect and utter
confidence of his mistress, honours came to him.
Riches in that age usually accompanied them.
He bought large estates, some in Lincolnshire, such
as the Manor of Deeping. He built hospitals, built
and endowed schools, and founded and supported
charities of all kinds. Lord Burleigh's hospital
can still be seen at the south-west corner of the
bridge at Stamford. He built a princely house,
entertained grandly, and kept a magnificent retinue
of liveried servants, and a staff of secretaries and
clerks. Yet the personal hand-work he got through
seems to have been marvellous. His arguments
" pro and con." on State questions, as submitted
for Elizabeth's decision, read like a " summing up "
on some intricate case by one of our modern judges—
no prejudice, no passion, the " for " in favour of any
one course on one side, the " against " on the other,
and the cold " dry light " of reason working out
what, on the whole, would be best. He kept
minute records of his estates, house expenses, cost
of clothing for servitors, down to the change in
colour of a ribbon, the pattern of a servant's badge
or the cut of a doublet, charities, wines, journeys,
and entertainments. He was a general referee for
nobles and landowners as to the management of

estates, the rotation of crops, valuation of buildings
and land, and looked after most of the details of the
rather numerous "progresses" of the Queen to
and from the great houses of her nobles, including
his own.   He was arbiter of disputes, recipient of
confidences, and a benefactor, to some extent, even
to his foes.   He could not interfere to save the
Duke of Norfolk's head, forfeited in one of the silly
conspiracies of the time (though on a previous
occasion he had got him released from the Tower),
but the Duke left the guardianship of his young son
to Cecil, in a letter from the Tower, as his doom
approached.   The men who plotted against Burleigh,
and were most "upset" by his shrewd diplomacy,
seem to have had a curious respect and good feeling
for him, as for some embodied genius of his country,
always to be reckoned with, and not personally to
be blamed for his inconvenient sayings and doings.
His one battle cry was "England," plus Elizabeth,
and the Reformed *Church* of England.   Long before
her accession, and during the dark days of Mary,
he had worked with the daughter of Anne Boleyn,
and when, on her accession, Archbishop Heath, with
some leading Councillors, went down to Hatfield to
hail the "Queen," they found Cecil already at her
side, and he was the first of the Council sworn.   One
chronicler relates that the lady went on her knees,
and with some fervour repeated, "*A Domino
factum est illud, et est mirabile in oculis nostris,*"
which was very orthodox and pious and proper of

her. But a person of her strong nature could scarcely be expected to always confine herself to the ecstatic language of the Psalms. Raking Cecil " fore and aft," as she did with her stinging tongue, and letting down his cherished little schemes every now and then with her freaks and her whimsies, she yet, on the whole, stood shoulder to shoulder with him, and worked manfully, as well as woman-fully, for her Realm and her people. She disliked Calvinists and Puritans as much as she resented the pretensions of Rome. She had a fine scorn for " rebels," and yet too much English common-sense to disregard legitimate discontent. *He* declined to bind himself either to " high " or " low," Puritan or priest, and, standing by the Monarchy and his mistress, could yet take heedful note of the wants of an expanding people. So, together, they sat on innumerable fences ; they tacked this way and that ; they " backed and filled " ; they made treaties to get out of some warm corner, and evaded them as the atmosphere grew cooler ; they temporised and threatened ; they denounced intrigues and conspiracies as something very wicked indeed, while they themselves intrigued and con-spired with the sheer human object of keeping body and soul together, and to that end their own heads on. When some of Cecil's combinations seemed going awry, perhaps through indiscretion of her own, she would " chip in " with some new foreign flirtation or a right royal rating to some Ambassador, whose schemes appeared to be riding full sail to port, and who, nonplussed and worried, was driven to cry out in the agony of his soul, and in something like modern Whitechapel, " Wot *is* her little game ? " Her Royal and other flames gave ample scope for this kind of " finesse." The Henrys of France, Charles IX., Eric of Sweden, Philip's son, Don Carlos, Don John of Austria, and others probably too " numerous to mention," formed the " state " or formal set of marionettes, to be advanced or withdrawn, cooed at or scouted, as " affairs " might require, whilst Dudley and Raleigh, Essex and Courtenay, were the more secular and privately loved dolls, to mention whom was to talk " scandal of Queen Elizabeth," but whose ups and downs were, nevertheless, made to work in very effectively with the mysterious issues of European politics. The flirtation with the Duc d'Alençon, ugly, pock-marked, and rising seventeen, the Queen being then a blushing damsel of thirty-nine, is too utterly funny even for our lightsome pen.

Space will not permit of more than a reference to *some* of Burleigh's " worries." His letter of advice to his son, for instance, " Use great prudence and circumspection in choosing thy wife, for from thence will spring your good or evil. It is an action of life like unto a stratagem of war (exactly !), wherein a man can err but once." This last was, of course, a slip. Men *have* married three or four times over, and " erred " every time, poor chaps, but Cecil's calm and mature judgment kept *him* all right in the matter of an able and accomplished second spouse. The anxious years during which his eldest boy Thomas was sowing his wild oats, and dragging his father's name in the mire, the dread crisis of the execution of Mary Stuart, the horrors of the St. Bartholomew massacre, and the deadly thrust at the very life of his country by the Spanish Armada, may well have seamed the statesman's brow and whitened his hair. He held out through it all till, at seventy-eight, full of years and honours, but presumably overborne by cares of State, his tough frame gave out, and his patient, indomitable spirit surrendered to the shadowy foe whom diplomacy could not outwit, and whose advances could not be fenced with. For a year or so he had been ill; the firm grasp was slackening; he had decanted much of his wisdom and the fruits of his long experience into the mind of his son Robert by letters and verbal advice, intending, no doubt, that that rising statesman should quietly slip into his place, as practically he did. Still they looked to him for strength and guidance, and amid the twinges of his implacable gout and a general sense of growing weakness, he still foiled intrigues, battled with the constant hankering of Essex and others to get the mastery of the Queen's will, and heard indifferently such snubs as that gracious lady could bestow, even in his physical helplessness. Following out his policy of peace, " if possible," though not

" at any price," he refused to back Essex in a projected war with Spain, and after a violent scene
between the two, the old Treasurer handed to the
Earl the Psalms, pointing to the line, " Bloodthirsty
men shall not live out half their days." Probably
Essex thought of this as he walked behind the
headsman on the morning of his own doom. Again,
Cecil had differed from the Queen, and, as usual in
any matter of real importance, refused to give way.
He left in a " huff," was persuaded to stay, but
refused, and the lady then delicately intimated
her opinion that he was a " froward old fool." At
last, for twelve days, he lay at Cecil House, in the
Strand, hard by the site of that grand Hotel Cecil
we now hear of. After a fit of convulsions he said,
" Now, the Lord be praised ! The time is come,"
sent for his children, told them to " Love and fear
God," and to " Love one another," prayed for the
Queen, handed his will to his steward, turned his
face to the wall, and died. The State funeral at
Westminster was a grand function, and the hard,
stern Elizabeth not only did him the honour of
" weeping " at his loss, but two years afterwards
it is recorded, " She doth wax weak since last
troubles, and Burleigh's death doth often draw
tears from her goodly cheeks."

CHAPTER IX.

"Bubble, Bubble, Toil and Trouble."

Henry, third of his name and fourth of his line, was a lad of nine, and, so far as such a child could be, was in league with his father's enemies, the Barons and the French. After John's ruin and death there was one notable fight at Lincoln, and then the boy King seems to have succeeded without serious question to the sovereignty of this troubled Realm. Gilbert de Gaunt had retreated from the siege of the Castle on hearing of John's march from Norfolk, but returned on what the joker of that day might have called the "turn of the tide." He was duly cursed and interdicted by the Pope, who now saw his way to favour the cause of the new King. But Gilbert "sat tight" around the Castle until the Regent, Earl Pembroke, raised a force and marched to the rescue. This he did in a manner that has been copied by actor managers in all succeeding years, and which entitles him to front rank as designer and organiser of spectacular drama. Each Noble, Banneret, or Squire was entitled to carry an ensign. By placing duplicates of these amongst the baggage and elsewhere in the

line of march on the approach to Lincoln, the Earl
created the appearance of double the force he
really had. It is difficult to understand how such
a simple trick can have imposed upon the old
campaigners who must, at least in some numbers,
have been amongst the English Baronial and
auxiliary French forces. The fact remains that
Fulke de Brent managed to get into the Castle and
sallied again thence, so as to get the so-called rebels
and their foreign friends between himself and
Pembroke's advancing ranks, with the result of a
crushing and decisive victory. Their chief leader,
the Earl of Perth, was slain by a lance thrust
through his helmet in the Cathedral yard, most of
the other chiefs were taken prisoners, with some
400 knights, besides esquires and crowds of the
ordinary " food for powder " sort, who take such
delight in these little discussions, and who always
get such an unaccountable disproportion of kicks
over " ha'pence." Many tried to escape in boats
down the Witham, but were drowned, and the rest,
flying in all directions, were put to death by the
country people, who seem, on the whole, to have
" stood for the King " (John) or whoever might be
his heir. This was the celebrated " Lewis Fair,"
so named in cynical remembrance of the French
Dauphin's share in it, and it was something upon
which all succeeding Louis' might reasonably
ponder when meditating any interference with this
Island or its inhabitants, their love of freedom,

their independence of spirit, their " dog goned "
capacity for hard hitting, and their general " cussed-
ness." The battle began at two o'clock, June 4th,
1218, and ended at nine. Old Matthew Paris
writes : " So expeditious were the merchants in
transacting business at this fair ! " One Geoffrey,
natural son of Henry II., by Fair Rosamond, and
who had been nominated by that monarch as quite
a proper person to be Bishop of Lincoln, took a
prominent part with many Lincolnshire Worthies
of those days and fought for " brother John " or
the heir. He always took to the field of battle
some stronger form of argument than the pastoral
crook, his object, of course, being to reach the
brains of his opponents by the most direct and
" penetrating " logic.

The Shire came not into any special prominence
in Henry III.'s time, although the reign extended
for fifty-six years. In 1241 he gave Boston to
Peter de Savory, Earl of Richmond, and his " heirs
for ever," so, of course, they hold it now, and the
worthy Mayor, no doubt, remits the tribute dutifully
either annually or on quarter days. We are not
aware of the address of the present Earl of Richmond,
but no doubt the Boston people have it. It must
have been a very " savoury " arrangement for the
Earl, considering the growing port dues, the fairs,
and the " soke," or money payment in lieu of feudal
service. The original expression here seems to have
been something like " soc," and probably some

impatient outbreak of the Earl's on not getting his collections in promptly has come down to us in the modern form of an exhortation to " pull up " one's " socks " at football, the final spurt of a rowing match, and the other vital movements of this whirling life. We need only, in passing to another and more virile reign, chronicle the fact that Henry was as grasping for money and as greedy for power as his father, that he, too, gave great way to the Pope, that he passed much of his life amid wars and rumours of wars, that he gave free scope to the family bad temper and vigorous language, but that his failings were redeemed by a certain religiousness and the pricks of a half-awakened conscience, the whole memory of the man being irradiated and, in a sense, glorified by the fact that in his reign that august institution the Parliament of England and the mother of all Parliaments took definite shape, and claimed, by the voice not only of Barons and Knights of the Shire, but of " Burgesses " from the towns, to advise, and if need be, control, the King and his surroundings in the proper government of these Kingdoms.

An example of this occurs in 1300-01, when King Edward I., sitting on the throne of his father, summoned a Parliament at Lincoln to consider the Pope's message forbidding the King from warring against the Scots. The Barons and the King decided that they had right, and, on their remonstrance to Rome, the Holy Father gave way.

Another record states that, in 1304, a Parliament
was again called at Lincoln, at which the inevitable
confirmation of Magna Charta was again exacted
before " other business " (the granting of funds)
could be gone into, and that the King held his
Court in that City " the whole of that winter." The
tall, fair-haired, ruddy *English* King had become
the wise, war-worn Monarch. Sixty-five battles
and sieges, harassing marches, Eastern crusades,
domestic fights with his Barons, and contentious
Parliaments at home were, for him, drawing to a
close. Scotch and Welch, Irish and French campaigns had left their mark upon him ; the cares of
a now powerful and growing State, and his labours
as law reformer and a sort of rough special providence to his people, must have tried the once
hardy and brilliant young prince. The violent
and somewhat brutal temper of young manhood
had given way to a generous forgiveness of injuries
and statesmanlike tolerance of the views of others.
But he could still give the Plantagenet bite, and
without overmuch of the bark. When the reply
to the Pope had been settled, Edward's announce-
ment was " By God's blood I will not hold my peace
for Zion, nor keep silence for Jerusalem, but I will
maintain my right." The " go between " for the
Pope was ruined, and presently banished, and his
Holiness elected not to " join issue." The story
of Edward's wife, Eleanor of Castile, and the sucking
poison from his wound, is now somewhat discredited,

and has no special reference to our Shire, except that she died in 1290, at Harby, near Grantham, of low fever, and the memorial crosses ordered by the King long existed at St. Peter's Hill, Grantham, and at Stamford, as marking the resting stages of that last progress to London, for final interment of a right royal lady and faithful loving wife.

In 1282, Boston and the surrounding country was submerged by a great flood. The monastery at Spalding was partly destroyed by the " vehemence of the wind and the violence of the sea." Many churches were destroyed, and the whole country there for the " most part turned into a standing poole, so that an intolerable multitude of men, women, and children were overwhelmed with the water, especially the Towne of Bostone or Buttolph's Towne, a great part whereof was destroyed." There were great fires and other calamities, the records of which are open to the curious and diligent reader. We also come across the fact that in the twenty-third of Edward I. (1296), Grimsby sent two Members to Parliament, and this our flourishing Lincolnshire port continued to do up to the Reform Act of 1832. The same may be said of Stamford and other Lincolnshire towns. In 1305 Edward granted to his second Queen, Margaret (sister of Philip of France), rich lands in and about Tattershall and the Manor of St. Botolph. He died in July, 1307, with a last injunction to his son not to bury his body until the Scots were finally conquered, but to carry his bones with the army till victory was finally assured, a grim way of finding the " dead hand " still something to do.   Old Froissart's record of him is "the good Kinge, Edward the First, was ryght balyant, sage, wyse and hardy, adbenturous and fortunate in all feates of warre and had much ado against the Scottes and conquered them iii or iiii tymes."

His tomb is in Westminster Abbey, where also lies Queen Eleanor, and on it is inscribed " *Eduardus primus, Scotorum Malleus, hic est Pactum Serva.*" Our stalwart and masterful northern brothers need not dwell resentfully on this.   They hammered *us* pretty handsomely on some occasions, and for many generations now we have fought " shouther to shouther " in all quarters of the globe for a glorious common Empire.   But Edward was no doubt Anglo-Saxon to the backbone of him, and justified the intention of his father in naming him after Edward the Confessor, with all that implied, and the hopes of his people, after 200 stormy years, in relying upon the advent, once more, of a King of their realm English born and bred.

About 1300, one of the most prominent men in the country was William de Gainsburgh, who, indeed, was Bishop of Worcester 1302 to 1308.   He was born at Gainsborough about 1250, took the Franciscan order, came under Edward's notice, was sent by him, in company with Hugh de Manchester, on a special mission to demand from Philip of France recompense for damages done by the French soldiery in Edward's province of Aquitain. He carried out this mission to the Monarch's satisfaction, and grew high in favour, but there is little record of his doings. He was so trenchant a supporter of the Pope and his "infallibility" that he urged "His Holiness ought never to be asked 'Why dost thou so?' though he causeth the damnation of thousands." Rather strong, but they didn't mince words in the 13th century.

There was also a "Richard de Gaynisburgh" (spell it just as you please!), who is said to be the same person who, under the name of "Richard de Stow," contracted with the Lincoln Dean and Chapter for the new work of the Cathedral. His monument within the Minster is well known.

It was in Edward the First's time that Hanseatic and Flemish merchants did a large trade in and out of Boston. Traders from Ipres, Cologne, Ostend, Caen, and Arras occupied houses in the town (1279), and a great annual fair or "Mart" was held. It is on record that the Canons of Bridlington attended this fair regularly for some thirty-five years for "wines, groceries, cloth, etc.," and there was a large revenue to the King from Customs.

H

CHAPTER X.

" THE ROD IS MY SIEVE."—DR. BUSBY.

THE greatest schoolmaster of the ages ? Well—er
—that is a rather large order, although he is so
held by many, but in view of Dr. Arnold, Dr.
Temple, and others, we desire to be guarded in our
judgment—besides, our printer is not overstocked
with notes of exclamation. But that he was a great
man you have proof (of a sort) in the fact that when
Charles II. visited Westminster School the Doctor
kept his hat on, and on that not very virtuous,
but good-humoured, monarch quietly asking the
reason, replied, " Sir, it would never do for the boys
to think there was any greater man than the
master ! "

Anyhow, he was the greatest *flogger* of his time.
He never spoiled a boy by sparing the rod, and if
his " system " had prevailed with other leading
pedagogues the nation must have gone in for
re-afforesting the land with birch in all available
districts, to be reared under the eye of whatever education department then existed. The normal supply
of those interesting twigs would have " run out."

DR. BUSBY.

He was *great* in his tenure of office, for he held the master's chair at Westminster for fifty-seven years, and he was great in results, for in hard on six decades he passed under his iron rule a whole army of the young generation of each, including Dryden (glorious John), who " found English poetry brick and left it marble," Philip Henry, John Locke, Christopher Wren, and other notables, not forgetting the thirteen English and Irish bishops who could look back and remember that in their tender youth they had imbibed their Latin and Greek from the good Doctor, and been guided in the ways of righteousness by that swift-descending switch. How curiously it reads now-a-days when a teacher mustn't box a boy's ears or give him a " hander " without having to record the punishment and reporting to some " Board " or other ! What *would* be said if some master or assistant master, " greatly daring," and a little out of his mind from continuous calls for reports, explanations, and cataracts of " averages," were to take down a bad boy's breeches and apply a sound birching to the sacred spot those breeches are intended to conceal ?

Busby was born in 1606 at the little village of Lutton, or Sutton St. Nicholas, being thus " projected " from the infinite unknown right into the stirring times of James I., Charles I., and the Revolution of 1648, the Protectorate of Oliver Cromwell, the Restoration and Reign of Charles II., James II., and six years into the reign of William III.

Little seems to be known of his early days. His parents were not in much of a position, but he was sent to Westminster School, in 1620, graduated at Christ Church College, Oxford, 1628, became tutor same year, and took his M.A. degree in 1631. He must have made much reputation in some seven years, for it was in 1638 he was appointed to the great charge of his life. He had certainly gained a name for amateur acting, as he had played a leading part in an Oxford play before Charles and Henrietta Maria, and with such brilliant success that it is recorded he actually thought of adopting the stage as a profession. How droll to think of the awful master of Westminster mistaking *his* way of life, donning the " sock and buskin," and subjecting himself to be treated by some beef-headed country magistrate as a " vagabond " ! No, we may not suppose his promotion to be due to his histrionic talent. Rather, we should say, ascribe it to the fact that he was " esteemed a great master of Greek and Latin and an orator."

He was but thirty-two when he took up the Master's ferule and undertook to guide the ways of some of the best young blood of the country. At thirty-three he was made Prebendary of Wells, and, after twenty-one years of hard work (1660), became Prebend of Westminster, also Canon and Treasurer of Wells, and took his degree as D.D. After that he studied and wrote (Archdeacon of Westminster, 1672), and taught (and thrashed) for thirty-five years with apparently unabated vigour, except during the few closing years, and in all that time he gave much in thoughtful charity, such as £5 a year towards the education of ten poor boys of Sutton and Gedney, Lectureships at Westminster, and help to widows and children of poor clergymen. His trustees for these latter benefactions meet to this day in the Jerusalem Chamber half-yearly, and it is pleasant to know that at the June meeting they, thirteen in number, and all " old Westminsters," dine together. Probably they sometimes spill the salt and cross the knives, but there is no record of the ominous number having interfered seriously with their digestions. The charities extend over three or four stated counties, his own being not forgotten.

During the whole gloomy time of the Revolution and the Protectorate he was conscientiously loyal to the Crown, and suffered for his consistency. In 1642 a Puritan mob attacked the Abbey, which some of the Westminster boys helped to defend, and that this was no mere " sky-larking " is shown by the fact that one " Wiseman," a knight of Kent (miscalled evidently in baptism), was killed by a " tile thrown from the battlements." A credible writer of the time testifies that on the day of Charles' execution he was prayed for by the assembled school an hour or so before his head was struck off. This kind of thing was not likely to please the party of " Praise God Barebones " and " Habakkuk Mangletext," and

Busby had to put up with the deprivation, in common with others, of his ecclesiastical holdings during the Long Parliament, but such was his repute as a teacher that he was allowed to continue as Master of Westminster, although, in a dispute which occurred with one of his assistants, Dean Owen, of Christchurch, and others took part against him ; the Dean, especially, taking occasion to remark that it would " never be well with the nation till Westminster School was suppressed." Busby had *his* turn at the Restoration, when he was appointed to carry part of the regalia at the coronation of Charles II., and was restored to his appointment.

There can be little doubt of the effect on successive generations of school boys produced by the Doctor's learning, piety, and stimulating zeal for their best interests. From all sorts and conditions of former scholars there came letters in after life testifying to the overpowering influence of the Master's personality upon their lives and careers. A few extracts may suffice : " The grave Busby, whose memory to me shall be for ever sacred ;" " Not only a master but a father and a real friend ;" " That which gained him my reverence was the greater sanctity of his life;" "There was an agreeable mixture of severity and sweetness in his manners." Sir Richard Steele writes that he had known great numbers of his scholars, and that " his genius for education had as great an effect upon the age he lived in as any philosopher, without excepting one, had upon his contemporaries." "He had a power of raising what the lad had in him to the utmost height in what nature designed him"; "There were no indifferent people come out of his hands, his scholars were the finest gentlemen or the greatest pedants in the age." Philip Henry, in his years of manhood, speaking of his old master, said, "The Lord recompense it a thousand-fold into his bosom."

On the whole, and with a side glance at the portrait still in the school, we get the idea of a grave, stern, studious figure, severe to a fault in discipline and school routine, sharply down on evildoers or idlers, but sympathetic and kindly helpful to any earnest, thoughtful boy who might require his guidance. But we might almost say his main characteristic has come down to us in the implicit belief he seems to have had in the efficacy of corporal punishment. He himself said, "The rod is my sieve, whoever cannot pass through that is no boy for me"; and again, "I see great talents in that sulky boy, and I shall endeavour to bring them out." The sulky boy was Robert South, who afterwards became a great preacher and a prominent State Church controversialist. Thos. Severne concludes his letter, "Lord! how I tremble to send this to you. I see you have me in awe still and ever will," but he subscribes himself, "Your first beloved scholar"; while Addison, in the *Spectator*, draws for us a neat cameo-like sketch of his standing before Busby's tomb in the Abbey, with Sir Roger de Coverly, and that worthy knight exclaiming, " Dr. Busby ! a great man ! He whipped my grandfather ; a *very* great man ! I should have gone to him myself if I had not been a blockhead ; a *very* great man ! "

Of a more contemporary incident than that of the fine old English gentleman, the creation of Addison's genius, we may say that the record is unfortunate for the " *raconteur* "—not Dr. Busby. Good old Sam Pepys says in his diary, under date May 3rd, 1667, " To Westminster by coach : the Cofferer (one Ashburnham) telling us odd stories how he was dealt with by the men of the church at Westminster in taking a lease of them at the King's (Charles II.) coming in, and particularly the devilish covetousness of Dr. Busby." This reads as though written in the same sort of haste as that in which David concluded that all men were liars. The Doctor was then sixty-two, not only a schoolmaster, but a dignitary of the Church, a trustee with others for its interests, a matter-of-fact and business-like as well as a learned man, at home in figures and accounts. He could probably hold his own with any Secretary of the Admiralty or other official from Charles the Second's rather unscrupulous *entourage*, and if " Government " or the Court, always hard up for cash, wanted to " negotiate " something out of the Church's pocket into its own, whether in " leases " or in any other matters, why Dr. Richard Busby was not exactly the man they should have tried. Pepys is not often spiteful in his gossip, but in this case he must not count as against the Master of Westminster. *We* read the note as merely a little petulant outbreak at finding the Doctor a hard nut to crack, and that what Pepys and his companion wanted to extract from him was " no go."

A trouble that once broke out between Busby and one of his assistants bulked largely at the time, and led to much reporting, minuting, and " memorialising," but now reads like a scene from a not very brilliant comedy. " Busby *versus* Bagshawe " carries with it the flavour of a popular farce of our young days, " Grimshaw, Bagshaw, and Bradshaw." Bagshawe was the second master, and strove to aggrandise his own position and to upset the Doctor with his governors. Bagshawe showed his fanaticism by sitting in the Abbey with his hat on. The Doctor rebuked him. Busby thought his deputy did not use the birch enough, and Bagshawe's dignity was outraged at having to teach " puny boys in the first and second form." The Doctor tried to keep his lieutenant under, and Bagshawe (just like an assistant master !) sneered at his principal's Greek. This, of course, was *absolutely* unbearable. The feud went on, but Bagshawe was eventually suspended by the governors, and Busby came out on top.

A glimpse of the way in which the Doctor was looked at may be got from an anonymous poet who, in 1711, wrote of one Doctor Friend, then master :

> " Ye sons of Westminster who still retain
>   Your ancient dread of Busby's awful reign,
>   Forget at length your fears, your panic end,
>   The monarch of this place is now a *Friend*."

And Matthew Prior, poet, ambassador, and intimate of the great, one of Busby's " old boys," idealises his old master thus :

> " So when at school we first declaim,
>   Old Busby walks as in a theme,
>   Whose prop supports our infant vein
>   And helps the rickets in the brain."

At eighty-nine the strong typical pedagogue with the steel wrist and the stinging switch succumbed, and the vital spark flickered out. We do not seem to have been told much of the last days or the final scene. Probably the old man would take due precautions against any gossipy details of his illness or the incidents of his " passing." He was scarcely the man to care to shine to posterity in a sensation scene, or to condone " fussiness," even in the case of a great Schoolmaster. But they buried him in the stately fane where sleep the best of England, together with the heroes and leaders of that " Empire," of which England is grudgingly admitted to be the " predominant partner." There also reclines his effigy in marble, in skull cap, magisterial robes, and with a broken quill in his hand, to indicate, we may suppose, a final period to all book writing, school account keeping, and Greek and Latin exercise correcting. The aquiline

BUSBY'S TOMB. (Westminster Abbey.)

[G.M.P.

nose, firm lips and chin, deep-set eyes, overhanging brows and high forehead, seem like nature's certificate to his right of entry into that august company. The hard white of the marble does not show so much sternness as simple determination and energy of character, tempered by kindliness. His eminent, and afterwards famous, pupil, Dr. Robert South, is beside him in the same material. The tombs of Tennyson and Browning are but a few feet off. The bust of Archbishop Tait nearly faces the Busby monument, from one of the time-worn pillars; Longfellow is near enough to glow in the same shaft of sunlight; Chaucer and Edmund Spenser are close by, and the fine bust of the Doctor's erewhile scholar, " glorious John " Dryden, seems almost gazing from a near angle across to the once dreaded " Master."

That the Doctor had a grim humour is manifest. A boy once found some plums in Busby's study, and in the Doctor's momentary absence ate some, saying, " I publish the banns of matrimony between my mouth and these plums. If any here present know just cause or impediment why they should not be united you are to declare it or hereafter hold your peace."   The Doctor had overheard, and next morning the lad was called up and " disposed " (horrible expression !) for punishment.   Busby took hold of his accustomed implement and said, " I publish, etc., between this rod and this boy. If any of you, etc., etc., ye are to declare it ! "   The victim

prepared for the sacrifice called out, " I forbid the
banns ! " and the Doctor for once hesitated.   " For
what cause ? " said he.   " Because," answered the
boy, " the parties are not agreed," and the master
let him off.   There is a story of the tables being
turned on him, but we don't believe it.   It may be
" *ben trovato*," but it is positively " too good to be
true."   An old " Westminster," who had often felt
the strength of the Doctor's zeal for discipline, but
who had gone to sea and risen to the command of a
fine frigate, invited Busby to visit his ship in the
Downs.   The Doctor accepted, but when he got up
the ship's side the captain cried out, " You (appalling
expletive) old scoundrel !   I'll pay you off now.
Boatswain ! give him three dozen ! "   But in most
cases, especially with his pupils, Busby " had the
best of it."   Father Petre, a noted ecclesiastic of
his day, former Westminster boy, and afterwards
pervert to Rome, met him one day in the Park and
spoke to him.   The Doctor professed not to recog-
nise him in that particular garb.   " After com-
pliments," as the foreign cypher telegrams have it,
the master exclaimed, " But, sir, you were of another
faith when you were with me.   How dared you
change it ? "   " The Lord had need of me," said
the priest.   " The Lord had need of you, sir !   I
have read the Scriptures as much as any man.   I
never knew the Lord had need of anything but
once, and then it was—an ass ! "   We should think
Petre became petrified.

We can't resist quoting one more apparently authentic story. A hot afternoon at Westminster, a crowd of boys playing in the yard, Busby correcting themes in the schoolroom—monitor sent down to stop the noise—little or no result. Some big boys then despatched to bring up the chief offenders. A fragile little Frenchman happened to be looking harmlessly on at the games, viewing the Abbey, and so on. Quite in the approved dare-devil public-school-boy style the stalwart lads seized the Frenchman and hauled him up to the master. " Horse him," said Busby, and when duly " disposed " for the occasion, the obnoxious alien was well flogged and then hustled out of the precincts. Bubbling over with rage and shame, monsieur wrote a challenge to Busby from a neighbouring coffee-house and sent it in by a street porter. When the Doctor read this missive he calmly said, " Fetch me a rod and horse this man ! " and the porter was then enabled to enter into full sympathy with his employer. When he got back and told the Frenchman of the inconvenient way in which the answer had been conveyed to him, and which it was only possible to transmit further by material method, the dumbfounded foreigner could only exclaim, " *C'est un diable !* "

The Doctor seems never to have married. He was not the sort of person to have prostrated his manly dignity and his pedagogic stateliness at the feet of some fly-away beauty, who would have worried him about new dresses, and have always been having her mother to stay with her, and if any *sensible* lady ever thought of *him* in that way she would, no doubt, on reflection cast a sheep's eye on that ferule, and wonder how far " dear Richard " might be tempted in the future to carry out the distich :

> " A woman, a dog, and a walnut tree,
> The more you beat 'em the better they be."

CHAPTER XI.

Ups and Downs of Kings.

Edward II., like his grandfather, Henry III., was not brought specially into connection with our county, except at rather long intervals, and for temporary purposes. He called a Parliament at Stamford in 1309, summoning " Earls, Barons, and tenants in chief by Knights' service " to meet him at Newcastle, with " horse, arms, and whole service," for another expedition to subdue the sturdy Scots. In 1314 he granted to Lincoln the inestimable boon of a " Mayor," receiving only, in certain coin and supplies, subsidies or " benevolences " in aid of his Scottish wars. Again, in 1326, there was a great gathering of Peers and Prelates at Stamford to discuss and advise with the King on sundry matters of Church and State. But this weak, vacillating, and " feckless " Prince, who dragged the Royal dignity at the tail of creatures like Piers Gaveston and the Despensers ; who had a disreputable Queen, capable of despising and hating her husband ; who was destitute of any genius for government, and who incurred the terrible humiliation of Bannock-

burn, met the frequent ending of a useless or mis-
chievous Sovereign in those rough days, and was
secretly murdered in Berkeley Castle, 1327, no
doubt by order of his Queen, Isabella, triumphant in
her alliance with the enraged nobles. We just
notice that at one time in his troubled reign he had
to assign the dues and customs of the port of Boston
in security for debts incurred for the supply of wine,
fish, and other edibles and potables required for
the Royal Household and at State banquets. The
echo of the dying shrieks of this hapless Monarch
along the gloomy corridors of that fateful fastness
have come down to us through the centuries, and
lend a pathetic touch to an otherwise useless and
ignoble career.

Then came, as though by natural alternation,
another *strong* man, of trenchant words and deeds,
and a virile, kingly reign of fifty-one years, with
occasional glimpses, for Lincolnshire, of a Knightly
Majesty, not before seen on the throne of these
Islands. Stained and faulty the record, no doubt,
but, on the whole, carrying forward the heavy
burden of English Sovereignty with Royal and
soldier-like dignity. He called a Parliament at
Stamford in the year of his accession, and granted
an assignment of one hundred marks per month
(say £66 to £67—not a very " Royal " allowance !)
for the maintenance of his miserable father, then
deposed, and still existing by the precarious tolerance of the Barons. Two Knights were told off

to look after and be responsible for the fallen King.
The following year a sort of Conference, not a
Parliament, was summoned at Lincoln, whereat
many high prelates and nobles took counsel with
each other and with Edward as to making peace
with the Scots, who were again harrying the border,
and making things "hum," under the Earl of
Moray, as far south as the Wear. Wars with the
Scots, wars with France, quarrels with Parliament,
squabbles about taxes and loans, pretty well filled
up Edward's time for the next twenty years, and
then (1348) there is an old record of a mighty rain
at Lincoln (and in many other parts of the country)
"from Midsummer to Christmas." All the lower
parts of the town were flooded, and, no doubt from
want of some modern drain pipes and a few active
sanitary inspectors, "the plague made such havoc
that the living could scarce bury the dead." Even
in the midst of this trouble, however, our old friend,
"labour," was beginning to have his say, for in
that same year the weavers of Lincoln obtained a
grant or Charter from Edward authorising them
to prevent any weaver not of their Guild from
working at his trade "within twelve leagues of the
city." This was cancelled a few years afterwards,
but the incident forms a nice quaint little premoni-
tion of the delightful "Trades' Union" regulations
under which we have to rub along in this 20th
century. In 1346 our little Grimsby, not then
having attained to "Great," furnished the King

I

for the siege of Calais with eleven ships and one hundred and seventy seamen. It must have been a fairly considerable port and fishing centre. As showing the growth of the place, or the increased exactions of State, the port in 1359 provided, for an expedition to Brittany, seventeen ships and three hundred and sixty-one men. Boston was twelfth on the list of eighty-two leading towns, only London, Bristol, Plymouth, and a few others topping her !

In Edward's time Stonyford, Steaneforde, or Stamford, came near to become a rival school, for younger Britain, to Oxford or Cambridge. A number of Oxford students, in course of some local disputes, gathered at Stamford and began to organise. Under a promise of redress of grievances they were ordered to disperse, and eventually, no doubt, returned to their old colleges. Their authorities there, however, exacted from them a declaration that they would not read or attend lectures at Stamford. Cambridge also took alarm, as the bigwigs there obtained a sort of guarantee from the King or Government that no other University than the two hitherto known should be recognised. The reputation of Stamford as a place of study, and the collegiate buildings there extant, bear out this story, and there is, or was till recent years, a " Dean." What had been hoped or expected may be gathered from a passage in Spenser's " Faery Queene," picturing the gathering of the rivers to

celebrate the marriage of the Thames with the
Medway :

> " And after him the fatall Welland went,
>   That if old sawes prove true (which God forbid!)
>   Shall drown all Holland with his excrement,
>   And shall see Stamford, though now homely hid,
>   Then shine in learning more than ever did
>   Cambridge or Oxford, England's goodly beames.
>   And next to him the Nene down softly slid ;
>   And bounteous Trent, that in himselfe enseames
>   Both thirty sorts of fish and thirty sundry streames."

With all the military glory of Edward's reign, his
often wise and far-seeing statesmanship, his tactful
adjustment of his own masterful temper to invincible
facts, and to persons necessary to his purposes,
and with the diplomacy which won him advantages
side by side with his arms, his long and strenuous
reign ended in a certain shame and sense of defeat.
His wretched subjection to the woman Alice Perrers,
the death of the Black Prince, his gallant warrior
son, and the loss of nerve, probably from advancing
age, brought failure at last upon his policy and his
wars. The strong right arm was now enfeebled,
and relaxed its grasp upon the no longer coveted
sceptre. The weakened brain gave up the weaving
of diplomatic cobwebs, and the once stalwart
Edward, a weary and disappointed old man, lay
down to die.

Again a weakling took up the symbols of authority
without ever having any real power. Edward's
grandson, Richard of Bordeaux, son of the Black

Prince, born, and by training and tastes, more
than half a French lad, came to the throne
when eleven years old, and, of course, was for
long years in the hands of Councillors, each of
whom had an axe to grind, if not several. The
poor fellow's troubled reign had only partially an
interest for our county. The two mainly picturesque
incidents of his career were the effective " sticking "
of Jack Cade by Lord Mayor Walworth, in Richard's
presence, and the wretched King's own murder in a
remote Yorkshire stronghold. But neither Smithfield nor Pomfret Castle were then, or are now, in
Lincolnshire. The old worries with the nobles
went on, mobs rebelled, and rioted against the
oppressive taxes. Richard made specious promises
but fulfilled none, and hadn't the wit, apparently,
to play off parties against each other, as some of
his predecessors had done, and as his powerful
conqueror, Bolingbroke, knew so well how to do.
Some of the incidents of our second Richard's
" forcible feeble " reign may be noted.

In 1385, four years before the King declared
himself of age and assumed full Sovereignty, one
John Walsh, a native of Grimsby, accused of high
treason by a certain gentleman of Navarre, Martileno de Vilenas, challenged his accuser to mortal
combat, and defeated him. The result of the fight
may not have satisfied the *judicial* mind of Mr.
Walsh's innocence, as truth cannot always guide
the right sword or spear thrust, especially if, as we

are often told, she keeps her incommodious habitation at the bottom of a well. Nor can " Justice," so long as she chooses to go about with a pocket handkerchief tied over her eyes, expect to see how to " touch the spot " she may aim at with the point of her own protégé's weapon, instead of allowing the innocent one to be " stuck " in his own perfectly virtuous stomach. In this case, Walsh's victory was complete, as the " furriner " was promptly hanged for " false accusation," and if Martileno de Vilenas was not satisfied, we must assume that he ought to have been.

It was in the following year that Richard came to Lincoln, and granted to the Mayor and his successors the privilege of having the sword of the Corporation carried before them in all processions and other public functions. Several Councils appear to have been held at Stamford in this reign, but notably one in 1392, which, not being, we suppose, a properly constituted " Parliament," conducted itself in the egregious manner " hereinafter following " : The " Lords and Chief Estates of the Realm," whoever that may have meant, were to decide as to peace or war with France, and, amongst other things, it turned out that " the Londoners," always a rather stiff-necked and contumacious lot, had not only refused the King a loan of £1,000 (a Plantagenet hard up for £1,000 !), but had nearly killed a " Lombard," who had offered to arrange the little " deal." The Council therefore " resolved " that, instead of a Mayor, London should, in future, " be governed by one of His Majesty's Knights, their privileges and liberties to be revoked, and their laws abrogated." Those who have read or heard anything of the stamp of men the Londoners used to choose for their Mayor and " Earldormen," may form a fancy picture for themselves of the short shrift that was given to that silly resolution by the hardy Cockneys, with their pikemen and archers, their " train " bands, their veteran campaigners, and their dogged defiance of anything like dictation or " dragooning."

Before the last grim scene of murder was enacted at Pomfret, poor wayward, passionate, heartbroken Richard is shown by Shakespeare as gracing the triumph and riding in the train of Bolingbroke, the Lancastrian usurper. In the " Tragedy of King Richard II.," the poet makes old York, the uncle of both Richard and Henry, report, with graphic force, the scene to the Duchess, his wife :

> .   .   .   " Rude misgoverned hands, from window's tops,
> Threw dust and rubbish on King Richard's head.
> .   .   .   .   The Duke, great Bolingbroke,
> Mounted upon a hot and fiery steed,
> Which his aspiring rider seemed to know,
> With slow, but stately pace, kept on his course,
> While all tongues cried, ' God save thee, Bolingbroke ! '
> .   .   .   .   .   .   Men's eyes
> Did scowl on Richard ; no man cried, ' God save him.''

A year or so after Richard's death, 1396, his uncle (York's brother), and uncle also of Henry of

Bolingbroke—John of Gaunt, the great Edward's second son—married one Katherine, widow of Sir Hugh Swynford, with whom he had already had irregular relations. There seems to have been a rather close connection with Lincoln in this case, as, in 1397, Gaunt built the Palace in the city so long known by his name. It is recorded that he spent considerable time at this place, and in Lincoln Castle, and with the Lord Abbot of Spalding, and often in the company of Geoffrey Chaucer, the reputed "Father of English Poetry," who, in fact, had married Gaunt's wife's sister. It was from the dying lips of "Old John of Gaunt" that the great poet made to issue those noble lines, so oft quoted, and of which we are all so proud :

> " This Royal Throne of Kings, this sceptered Isle,
> This earth of Majesty, this seat of Mars.
> This other Eden, demi-paradise ;
> This fortress built by nature for herself,
> Against infestion and the hand of war ;
> This happy breed of men, this little world ;
> This precious stone set in the silver sea."

CHAPTER XII.

Sir Isaac Newton.

THE world of human nature is but one vast museum of anomalies and curiosities. If some great man has not already said this he ought to have done, and we make some coming genius a present of this profound reflection, on which he can build up at least three volumes of original thought. We only bar a few of the so - called literary people of the day, who grub amongst the books of other writers and pick up a grain here and there of something like wisdom, as a barn-door hen pecks her matutinal barley, and with much about the same hungry avidity ; retailing the promiscuous and diluted philosophy as original matter for the already gorged stomach of the half-penny newspaper reader.

Who would think that one of the greatest natural philosophers and discoverers the world has seen was roused from boyish inertness and a certain tendency to " frittering," and set definitely upon his life pathway of profound scientific investigation, by a school fight ? Yet this was about the case of Isaac Newton, of whom James Thomson, poet of

The House in which Sir Isaac Newton was Born

"The Seasons" and "The Castle of Indolence,"
wrote :

> "First our solar system he surveyed
> With accurate ken, and by the mingling power
> Of gravitation and projection saw
> The whole in silent harmony revolve.

>   *   *   *   *

> "Then, breaking hence, he took his ardent flight
> Through the blue infinite ; and every star
> Which the clear concave of a winter's night
> Pours on the eye, or astronomic tube,
> Far stretching, snatches from the dark abyss ;
> Or such as further in successive skies
> To fancy only shine, at his approach
> Blazed into suns, the living centre each
> Of an harmonious system."

He was born on Christmas Day, 1642, in the old
manor at Woolsthorpe, a few miles south of Grantham, and so small and fragile was the infant that
his mother afterwards said she could have " put
him in a quart pot." It is quite as well for his
fame and the interests of human science that she
did not try. He was descended from the elder
branch of the Newton family, lords of the manor of
Woolsthorpe, and who had held the estate two
hundred years or so. He was extremely delicate
in childhood, so that a lady relative tells how, on
one occasion, she went for the doctor, not in the
least expecting on her return to find the boy alive.
As a growing lad his health continued precarious,
but close and loving attention, with a strict dietetic
regimen, gradually strengthened the frail body, and

enabled it to bear the strain of the gigantic intellect it was destined to develop.

From the first he was quiet, not gloomy, thoughtful, not morose, studious, yet cheerful and companionable. He soon got all that the village school could give him in the way of erudition, and at the age of twelve was sent to the public school at Grantham, in which town there is now a fine bronze statue of him. In the mere technicalities of school life he seems for some time to have made but indifferent progress. Doubtless he was pondering many things. He stood low in the class, and seems to have had, on the whole, a certain contempt for " book-learning." It is related that when he looked first at some of the least obvious of the propositions of Euclid he expressed wonder that any human being should have thought it worth while to write down " problems " the solution of which was so simple. He evidently preferred to give his mind more to the making of water clocks, windmills, and a crude sort of velocipede. He made kites with tails scientifically adjusted by length, the number of notches, etc., to the pressure of atmosphere or force of wind against which the kite had to rise, and he constructed sundials at his lodgings, and other places, in accord with the latitude of the town, and " Isaac's dial " became the time guide for the people. When at home from school he would continue these mechanical and experimental pursuits, with the addition of making

fancy little tables and other " knick-knacks " for one
or two young lady playmates, with whose society
he appears to have been more suited than with most
of his boyish companions.   Indeed, one of these
ladies, after being twice a widow and having succeeded in living to eighty-two, confessed coyly that
she believed Isaac had been in love with her.   She
was not destined to play the part of Rebecca, for
Newton never married.   The story is that at the
time such connection might have been possible
the narrow means and uncertain position of the
young philosopher prevented the coming about of
anything definite.   We should say quite as much
prominence might be given to his frequent, if not
constant, absorption in the deep things of science,
and to the natural tendency of his spirits to rise
above such very mundane and common-place ideas
as being " in love " and " getting married."   Anyhow, the pensive reflections of a lady of eighty-two
as to somebody having been in love with her at
sixteen or eighteen are not always to be accepted
as " canonical."

At Grantham School came the fight already
referred to.   Accidentally or not, one of his school-
mates, a bigger boy than himself, and somewhat
aggressive, kicked Isaac in the stomach, and, no
doubt, urged on by the cheerful enthusiasm of
British lads for a fight, no matter how or with
whom or for what, the " ordeal by fist " was arranged,
the master's son most kindly and efficiently over-

looking the preliminaries and helping to keep the
ground. Newton licked the bigger boy, and when
the latter said he had had enough and owned he
was beaten, the young savages around cried, " Now
rub his nose against the wall," this operation being,
apparently, with the pugnacious youth of that time,
a sort of a free translation of the " *Væ victis* " of
more classic times, an insular form, in fact, of the
cultus of the " Caudine Forks." It is not stated
whether the nose was really rubbed or not ; massage
of that sort could not be continued for long, or the
feature would tend to disappear altogether ; but
Newton held his antagonist's face to the wall
sufficiently well to certify his own status of conqueror, and to gratify the passion for etiquette in
his schoolfellows. Now this boy had hitherto
beaten Isaac in the school-work ; but from this
time the latter began to ponder a problem which
had not yet presented itself to him. " Physically
I am better than he ; I am his master. Mentally,
he is better than I ; he is *my* master. Which is
preferable ? Surely I am still the inferior ! "
And he forthwith brushed up his " book-learning,"
went on by little leaps and bounds, took the wind
out of his late opponent's sails, and finished by
beating him at his books too.

By the time he was fifteen Grantham could do
no more for him, and there is a touching little scene
of the good old master calling Newton into the
midst of his schoolfellows, and with tears in his

eyes taking leave of his most promising pupil.
His mother wanted him at the farm, and he dutifully
went, but the position was, as our French neighbours
say, *impossible*. When he " attended market " he
would steal off to a quiet little room he knew of,
where were some old books, bottles containing some
of the choicest vintages of scientific lore, and in
these he would revel, oblivious of the price of corn,
or as to whether the turnips wanted rain or not.
The sheep went " every one his own way," and the
cattle had a high time with some of the growing
crops. Master Isaac would be under a hedge with
a book, or cogitating a mathematical problem. On
the very day when the grim Protector Oliver was
passing away to the wild music of the great storm
that swept over the country, Newton was curious
to test the force of the gale ; he jumped as far as
he could with the wind, then jumped against it,
and measuring his jumps and calculating the
momentum of his body, proceeded to compute the
actual wind pressure—the sweetest thing in scientific
acumen plus athletics we have yet heard. One of
his amiable biographers suggests, with diffidence,
that this may have been the origin of the phrase
" jumping to a conclusion," but we cannot, of
course, speak with authority on the subject.

The inevitable arrived : his mother and other
friends decided that Isaac Newton would never
make much of a farmer, and had better have his
free scope at college, and he was admitted at Trinity

in 1660 at the age of eighteen. There, of course, he made great headway, falling in with kindred minds, and sharpening his own mental apparatus by contact with that of others ; but not until 1665 did he take his degree as B.A., returning to Woolsthorpe in 1666 to avoid contact with the plague then raging. It was then that occurred the famous incident of the falling apple in the garden or orchard of the old home, which gave him a clue to his great discovery, and to a vast system of law which regulates alike the falling of a single leaf in autumn and the orbit of Uranus or Neptune. Copernicus was the first to trace that our planetary system moved round the sun ; Galileo proclaimed the movement of our earth as an established fact ; Newton penetrated the loftiest secret of nature : he found *why* these revolving satellites so moved, and to that extent, with reverence be it said, he divined and entered into the very thought of the Eternal.

It is stated authentically that at this time, when he was but twenty-four or twenty-five, he had by him all the materials for his massive work of the "Principia," and many other of the writings which were to follow. Henceforth his intellect advanced with majestic stride, until by almost universal acclaim it assumed the throne of science. And it showed itself as varied as it was profound. His chief work came to be the "Text Book of Cambridge." His views were fiercely controverted by Descartes, but the great Frenchman eventually gave way. Laplace, Herschell, and the rest have followed on his lines. He wrote well in French and Latin, and a mere list of the subjects he dealt with is enough to "stagger humanity" in a way never contemplated by Mr. Kruger. Silver Money, the Binomial Theorem, the Doctrine of Fluxions, Catoptrics and Dioptrics, the Trinitarian Doctrine, the Articles of Faith, the Chronology of Ancient Kingdoms, the Quadratures of Curves and Analysis of Equations by an Infinite Number of Terms, the Greek text of the New Testament, the Being of God, Optics, Telescopes, and the Book of Daniel, and, in moments of leisure we may assume, an annotated and illustrated complete system of Geography. He was appointed Master of the Mint in 1695, and was not too proud to bring his keenness and profundity down to practical questions of the currency. In 1703 he was chosen President of the Royal Society, and held that high position for twenty-three years and until his death. In 1705 Queen Anne had the honour of Knighting him. He sat in the legislature to defend the Universities against the encroachments of James II., and again for several sessions of a succeeding Parliament. He was one of the few men of genius who were appreciated by their contemporaries, instead of being left to the slack-baked and perfunctory attentions of posterity.

In spite of his early weakness he lived on to eighty-five, with but little bodily pain until within about twenty days of his death. He never had to use spectacles, and only lost one tooth in his life. (Dentists and opticians were not then the flourishing creatures they are now.) He had suffered from a well-known internal disorder, but not, it is recorded, to any serious extent. A violent return of this was brought on by his imprudently attending the meeting of the Royal Society as President, but when brought home he, between the paroxysms, conversed freely and even cheerfully with those about him until he sank into unconsciousness, from which there was no recovery. He died March, 1727. There was only one resting place for the casket which had held so great a mind. He was buried in Westminster Abbey, and although no pageantry could enhance his fame, every honour that men consider of value was paid to him. The Lord Chancellor, two Dukes, and three Earls were his pall-bearers. The monument in the Abbey witnesses to the feeling of his generation, and an eminent French writer remarked at the time, "We must go back almost as far as the ancient Greeks if we would find a like instance of so great a veneration paid to learning."

In one respect Newton was not quite free from an ordinary weakness of philosophers. We heard much recently of the "Absent-Minded Beggar." Absent-minded men of genius are always more or less in evidence. Sir David Brewster tells a story, not absolutely vouched for, of Dr. Stukely calling on Newton. He was shown into the dining-room and kept waiting. The table was laid, and Stukely, lifting the one cover, disclosed an inviting looking chicken. He grew impatient, then a little nettled, and finally sat down and ate the chicken, replacing the cover over the skeleton. At last Newton came in with apologies, and, continuing to converse, lifted the cover. He replaced it gently, remarking, "How absent minded we philosophers are! now, I really thought I had not dined!"

With all his vast acquirements and the breadth of his intellect he never seemed to raise himself above the common humanity around him. He was a consistent Churchman, but with no prejudice against Nonconformists. He studied the Bible habitually, maintained an humble faith in the Divine government, was opposed to anything like pomp or show for show's sake, although he could be dignified enough when stately ceremonial observances were necessary. His emoluments were ample, but he never hoarded. He gave away largely in his lifetime, holding that to leave money to others when we can ourselves no longer hold it, is "no true gift." He was very sensitive to cruelty, especially to animals, and a sad story of any kind would move him to tears. He must have been very self-contained and self-sufficing, as in youth he had but little help from the higher class of scientific books, and little of friendly counsel to guide him, whilst, later, the very wealth of his own mental resources must have

K

insured for him much of the isolation which is the penalty of genius.

As to the summing up of his life, most of us have heard of his own view of the incompleteness of his labours, and his discoveries. It is as well known as George Washington's cherry tree, but a little less problematical. We will not maim it by partial quotation, but give it in full and in the Master's words : " I do not know what I may appear to the world, but to myself I seem to have been only like a boy playing on the sea-shore, and diverting myself in now and then finding a smoother or prettier shell than ordinary, whilst the great ocean of truth lay all undiscovered before me." This was the Sage of Science, diffident and unobtrusive to the last. The inscription at Westminster Abbey fitly conjoins his mental and spiritual position with his blameless life : " He asserted in his own philosophy the Majesty of God, and exhibited in his conduct the simplicity of the Gospel."

NEWTON
Qui genus humanum ingenio superavit

THE STATUE, TRINITY COLLEGE, CAMBRIDGE.

om a Photo by]

[E. CLENNETT, *Cambridge*

CHAPTER XIII.

THE THREE HENRYS.

IT may be noted that the Bishop of Lincoln at
the accession of Henry IV. was Henry Beaufort,
the new monarch's half-brother, whom he afterwards
translated to Winchester, and who also blossomed
into the dignity of Cardinal. He was more than
once Chancellor of the Kingdom.

There is record of a curious incident connected
with Crowland Abbey as being in the advowson
or patronage of the Crown through Henry's heirship
to John of Gaunt. This " overlordship " extended
down to the great " dissolution," under Henry VIII.
Prior John, in 1494, received an " order of Court "
regulating the execution of felons. The Bailiff of
Spalding was to " conduct the malefactor from the
monastery prison to the gallows or place of execution,
the Bailiff of Weston should carry the ladder, the
Bailiff of Pinchbeck find the rope, and the Bailiff
of Moulton should therewith do the execution in
hanging the felon."   If the " malefactor " happened
to have any sense of the great Apostle's ideas as to
all things being done " decently and in order,"

these elaborate and kindly precautions must have soothed his last moments.

Henry IV., though born in Lincolnshire, appears not prominently in the county annals, nor is there much of court pageantry or warlike " alarums and excursions " to record even amid all the deadly struggle of the " Roses," except that particular reference is made to Stamford, which suffered much between the contending factions, being ravaged on one occasion by an army of Lancastrians, under one " Andrew Trollop," (which again sounds like a name we have heard something of in Lincolnshire). Camden holds that the town was so badly mauled as never to have recovered its former appearance, but this may be taken " *cum grano*." Anyhow, Stamford seems to have been Yorkist in its proclivities, and to have been " paid out " accordingly by the Lancastrians when they got the chance. The old and somewhat weary story of Irish stew, Welsh rarebits, and Scotch broth (well hot !) went on, and Bolingbroke, worried and diseased, his ambition gratified, but in constant dread of plots, rebellions, and assassination, plodded his lonely, weary way through the purgatory then called being " King of England." He died in 1413, and Harry of Monmouth, the ideal British King, and the darling " Prince of Wales " of our great Shakespeare, took up the sceptre. He, too, had little to do with Lincolnshire, and although his reign was summed up as " glorious," the tide of battle and the storm of great events swept over France and some parts of our own country, but not " the *county*."

He died after almost exactly nine years of sove-reignty, and the baby Henry, his only son and Sixth of the name, succeeded to a gruesome inherit-ance. It was in *his* boyhood, at nine years, that we read of the death, at Sleaford Palace, of Richard Fleming, Bishop of Lincoln, who had been nominated Archbishop of York by Pope Martin, but, as the Chapter refused to accept the translation, the Pope revoked his bull and the Bishop returned to his old diocese. Another instance, probably, of the per-sistent attitude of the Anglican Church in checking Papal pretensions. Bishop Fleming was the founder of Lincoln College, Oxford, but his work was ably furthered and consolidated by Beaufort aforesaid, and by Thomas Rotherham, a succeeding Bishop of Lincoln.

About midway of the long reign of the monk-like and half imbecile Henry VI. (1446), he held his court in the Bishop's palace on the hill at Lincoln, and four years later he spent three days and nights in Lent at Croyland Abbey, pleased with the devout-ness of the brothers, and desirous of being admitted to their order. He gave them certain privileges under the name of a " charter of liberties," but this was promptly revoked by his conqueror and successor, Edward of York. During the long fight between the White and Red the good brothers and

their Abbot had to keep a sharp look out for raids
upon their wealthy domain. They seem to have
pretty well "held their own," although on one
occasion a Lancastrian army was within six miles
of the Abbey, but this was met and dispersed by
Edward. The curious thing seems to have been
that whereas the monks, being still of the Old
Testament order of Christians, fortified their holdings and were prepared to fight fiercely for their
own, the monarch, still claiming to reign, instead of
being "every inch a king" and warrior, and prepared to defend his crown on the basis of "*Dieu et
mon droit*," abhorred bloodshed, yielded to almost
the least show of "*force majeure*," and amid all the
turmoil of a distracting and calamitous contest,
bore himself like a refined and cultured lady, horror-
struck at the enormities going on all about him,
and anxious only to preserve in full and vivid glow
the aureole of saintship already gathering around a
marred and ascetic visage.

In 1467 there was another great flood in the
" Parts of Holland," with much foreboding of evil,
as well there might be in those times, showers of
blood (? saturated red dust), armies fighting in the
air, a vision of St. George with his red cross in the
sky, and other matters likely to be observed by the
non-critical, especially when primed with strong
ale at the village " pub " or the " good wine " of an
abbey refectory, seasoned by an infusion of partisan
fanaticism. It was at the time of one of the occasional

quarrels between the weak King and the great Earl
of Warwick, and Henry in alarm went pilgrim to
St. Edmund, at Norwich, thence by Lynn and
Wisbeach to Croyland again, into which he came
with a " suit of 200 horse." The record says he
stayed there (no doubt at the abbey) for one night,
and walked next day through the town to the stone
bridge.

One didn't quite know in those days whether one
was King of England or not. The Yorkist monarch
found himself unpleasantly near to a big gathering
of rough-handed barons of the Lancaster persuasion, given to bad language and thirsting for Yorkist
blood. The Yorkist sovereign bolted. Then he
got *his* men together somewhere, and away scuttled
the Lancastrian King, giving vent, as he ran, to
ejaculatory and not very coherent remarks. Not
only in our shire, but all over the country, the
game of " topsy-turvy "-cum-" hide-and-seek " went
on—Guy, Earl of Warwick, playing his own little
part of " king maker," and balancing, as " Jack,"
this mighty game of " see-saw," while the virago
wife of Henry, Margaret of Anjou, shrilled and
cursed, stabbed and ravaged with the best (or the
worst) of them, and fought like a she wolf for the
rights of her cub, the young Edward of Lancaster.
Meantime the fair fields of England were drenched
with the blood of her best and bravest, and the
people, harried and plundered, hacked about by
men-at-arms, burnt out of their homes, half stupefied

in the general chaos, and deafened by the rude artillery of the times, could only stare with hopeless eyes into the thick darkness, and pray for *some* sort of dawn.

Shakespeare has lavished some of his most beautiful passages in " Henry IV." Long years after his usurpation, the King, in his sick chamber, is made to envy the sailor boy and the commonest of his subjects the divine gift of sleep, and to cry :

> "Uneasy lies the head that wears a crown ! "

and again :

> " Oh ! Heaven, that one might read the book of fate,
> And see the revolution of the times ! "

Yea ! Henry Bolingbroke was spared the last retributory curse of seeing, as in a vision, the consequences of his acts in the prolonged horror of the Wars of the Roses. Is it entirely a gracious providence that hides from *us* the after results of *our* acts, or are we to assume that, were it otherwise, the planet would be peopled with a dwindling race of melancholy and foreboding lunatics ?

CHAPTER XIV.

JOHN WESLEY ("THE WORLD IS MY PARISH").

WE, to whom the name of John Wesley is familiar as one of the household words of daily life, can scarcely realise that he has been *dead* more than a century. Born (1703) into the world of Queen Anne, of Louis XIV., and Marlborough, of Harley and of Bolingbroke, his childish ears must have rung with the echoes of Blenheim and Malplaquet, and the early doings (or misdoings) of Sir Robert Walpole. In his budding manhood he must have noticed, with more or less of interest, the literary career of François Marie Voltaire. The man who was to "turn the world upside down" on religious subjects, as did his prototype St. Paul, lived through the generations that witnessed the Act of Union with Scotland, the separation of the American Colonies, the memorable Siege of Gibraltar, and the Coalition Ministry of Lord North. He saw the first lowering of that revolutionary hurricane which drove France into delirium, struck to death a King and Queen of ancient line, and swept, tornado like, over Europe. Amid all the "hurly burly" of

that old-time world, this little child, born in a remote
Lincolnshire parsonage (Epworth), and only one of
a numerous family, was destined to conceive, to
initiate, and to organise a spiritual work which has
resulted, up to now, in a "communicant" fellow-
ship of 6,000,000 men and women, 40,000 Ministers,
and congregations, all over the known globe,
amounting to 25,000,000 ! This is scarcely exceeded by the more immediate work of Martin
Luther himself, as recorded in the statistics of the
Lutheran Churches of Prussia, Denmark, Sweden,
Norway, and other States of the Continent.

We need not repeat here much that is told of
Wesley's young days, of his godly father and mother,
of his rigorous training, the timely culture of his
infant faculties, and of his being rescued at the age
of six as a "brand snatched from the burning"
flames which were devouring the Rectory. Perhaps,
however, all Lincolnshire people do not know that
on one occasion he heard his father's clerk give out :
"Let us sing to the praise and glory (etc.) an hymn
of my own composing " :

> King William is come home, come home,
> King William home is come ;
> Therefore together let us sing
> The hymn that's called T'dum !

As a boy he was very desirous of being logical,
and of having a "reason for everything." In
dealing with this tendency, his wise father once
said, "Child, you think to carry everything by

dint of argument! You will find how very little is ever done in the world by close reason," and his own comment, long afterwards, was "little enough!"

He got a presentation for the Charterhouse, and there earned a scholarship for Oxford, whence (about 1720), he wrote his mother, "I propose to be busy as long as I live," a youthful aspiration most marvellously fulfilled. He got work as tutor, was elected fellow of Lincoln College (1726), and two years afterwards (1728) was admitted to priest's orders. He seems to have "scaled off" the incipient "positivism" of his early days, and taken on some of the asceticism and dreamy enthusiasm of the mystic. He had read Thomas à Kempis and Jeremy Taylor, and talked over with his father and mother the "Imitation of Christ" and "Holy Living and Dying," as related to the actual responsibilities of a modern Christian. He was "well bred," as proved by his collateral relations with the Wellesleys, but a certain strain of Puritan blood may have engendered in him a desire to make practice accord with profession, a thing singularly *out* of accord with the then state of things in the religious world.

Returning to Oxford, after assisting his father in the sub-charge of the little village of Wroot, he found a small society already formed, of his brother Charles and other earnest young men, who had established for themselves a "method" of living considerably nearer the standard of the early disciples than the ordinary clerical ideal of those days. They had already begun to be called " Methodists," and seem at once to have recognised in John a natural leader, and, the party being joined by George Whitefield, the movement took shape, and went on for five or six years amid scoffs and jeers and brow-beatings manifold. Then came the offer from the founders of the Colony of Georgia that John should go out to preach the Gospel to the settlers and Indians, and, after much inward debate, he decided to accept, and his brother Charles determined to go with him.

They sailed in October, 1735, with two others of their little Methodist Company, and in due course arrived and set about their Mission. There is no clear record, however, of any specific success therein, and the main result of the expedition seems to have been a further development of Wesley's peculiar and complex character. He who had " gone to convert others " had discovered that he himself had " never been converted," and he gave the rather tame reason for relinquishing the work that there was " no possibility of instructing the Indians," neither had he found or heard of any Indians who had " the least desire of being instructed." He had apparently laid upon the settlers a burden too grievous to be borne in restriction of enjoyments and general asceticism of life. He had resented the legal application of certain local objections to his religious régime, and had, in appearance at least, fled from Justice. He had become entangled, through no fault of his own, we fain believe, but through the innate simplicity and "gush" of his temperament, with a young lady, and had incurred the ill-will of her uncle, one of the principal men of the colony. In principle and practice his "method" as a clergyman of the Church of England had been distinctly "high." He refused to baptise babies except by cold immersion, the child in one instance being but eleven days old. He would not accept sponsors unless known to be communicants. He insisted upon severe fasting and "confession" before Communion, nor would he read the Burial Service over the body of a dissenter. On the other hand, he had gone through perils and privations by "flood and field," he had travelled and worked incessantly, and the constant introspection to which he subjected himself (too morbidly, as some will hold) had gone on, narrowing his mind in one direction, widening it in another, towards the formation of a character almost unique in history, and made up of hallelujahs and groanings and tears, nervous self-distrust and confident command of others, minute questionings of the acts and motives of his friends and associates in the most private details, and melancholy failure in his own domestic life, passionate attachment to the creeds and formularies of the National Church, and more than a sneaking kindness for hysterical and cataleptic manifestations of the "Spirit," which that Church held with scorn to be but the outcome of bodily disease, gross imposture, or sheer lunacy. In organisation, extremely careful and "matter-of-fact," he yet habitually referred for guidance to the opening of the sacred volume at a particular verse, and while keeping nearly all his life an exact account of receipts and expenditure, he gave away monies in all directions as fast as he got them. He had absorbed much mystical theology from William Law and the leaders of the "Moravian Brethren," and yet had studied with strong sympathy the Meditations of Marcus Aurelius and admired Ignatius Loyola !

It was not till February, 1738, when he was back in London, after nearly suffering shipwreck on the voyage home, that, at an obscure meeting in Aldersgate Street, listening to Martin Luther's preface to the Epistle to the Romans, he felt his "heart strangely warmed," and experienced the process which his followers call "conversion," and which the American negro sings and dances about when he has "got grace." This meant that the theory of life was, for him, radically changed, that everything was to be seen from a new point of view, and that action *must* follow upon conviction, or life itself be deemed a failure and a wreck. Thenceforth, the work of his manhood, his prime, and of his trembling old age, was to be that of a prophet or "Forth Teller," he must declare to the people of his own land, and, by deputy, to the people of *all* lands, the things of the Spirit which he not merely believed, but which he knew, and this to go on till he might truthfully take up almost the very words of the great Apostle himself, "In journeyings often, in perils of rivers, in perils of robbers, in perils from my countrymen, in perils from the Gentiles, in perils in the city, in perils in the wilderness, in perils in the sea, in perils among false brethren; in labour and travail, in watchings often, in hunger and thirst, in fastings often, in cold and nakedness." Slandered and persecuted, hustled and stoned, haled before unjust judges, over England, Scotland, Ireland, and Wales, in cottages of the peasantry, and in attics and cellars of city workers, by night and by day he rode horseback or tramped afoot through storms of hail and rain, through fen mists and northern snow drifts, until at "eventide it was light," the handy stone was left on the roadway, the effective bludgeon was held down, the "skirl" of sneers and sarcasm died slowly away, and the tired, but still cheerful, old evangelist lay down to rest in utter peace.

As his fellow clergy refused to open their pulpits to him, he made his first effort as an open-air preacher at Bristol, to a concourse of 3,000 people, mainly of the poorer class, and from that time his penetrating powerful tones were waited for for hours in all weathers and in all places by gatherings of ten to twenty and even thirty thousand people.

To realise how this came about one must glance

at the state of religion, and especially of the National
Church, during the first quarter of the 18th century
and the few following years. Whitgift, whose
career we have already dealt with, lived through
a mighty period of struggle and controversy as to
which form of Christianity should prevail. Wesley
came into a world which, when it turned at times
from its " primrose path of dalliance " with dissipa-
tion, heavy drinking, and debauchery, discussed
with graceful indifference whether there should be
any Christianity at all. As a means of developing
and guiding the spiritual forces of the nation, the
Church was dead, dead as Queen Anne has ever
since been.

It was used by so-called statesmen, with cold
and congenial irony, as an engine of political power.
It could consistently use in this way the services
of a Jonathan Swift, and reward him with a Deanery.
Conviction had been silenced, the pulpit had lost
its influence, a large proportion of the clergy lived
in extreme poverty, many others lived notoriously
disreputable lives, discipline was neglected, and
pluralities and the " cure of souls " by absentee
rectors and vicars were shamefully prevalent.
Bishop Newton, of Lincoln, in complaining of the
largeness of his diocese, seems to have made it a
pretext, not so much for a suffragan, or some help
in his spiritual work, as for more " pay." Canon
Overton of Lincoln, Rector of Epworth, looking
back upon it, could write : " The Church partook

CITY ROAD CHAPEL, LONDON. (John Wesley's Chief Centre.)

[G.M.P.

of the general sordidness of the age. It was a time of great material prosperity, but of moral and spiritual poverty such as scarcely finds a parallel in our history."

We can change the metaphor, and say that the frozen and apparently sterile soil bore within it the seeds of a coming spring. The stern morality and rugged devoutness of Dr. Johnson, the saintly sweetness of Fletcher of Madeley, the life work of John Newton, and the simple, emotional piety of Cowper, were to pierce through the hard surface of 18th century rationalism, the heralds of a great revival. When Wesley began his work he " fluttered the Volscians " who lived in fat rectories or drew handsome revenues from distant benefices. They scoffed and stormed alternately, and in many cases worked openly for his destruction, but nothing availed against his indomitable pluck, his untiring energy, his constitutional strength of body, and his abiding sense of " guidance from on High."

There is a quaint story of one of Wesley's services at Bath (1739) being interrupted by the celebrated (or notorious) Beau Nash, who demanded his authority for his proceedings as an itinerant preacher. John's answers, however, were so pungent and to the purpose that the master of revels and reigning fop of the period retired in confusion, faultless outfit, white beaver, and all.

For about forty-five years Wesley carried his message up and down his native county at intervals

L

of one or two years, his first visit being to Epworth
when near thirty-nine years old (1742). He was
not allowed to preach in his father's parish church,
but stood on his tombstone as he discoursed to a
large crowd. He held a further service the following
Sunday at Haxey, and again in the same place to
a " vast multitude gathered from all parts." Up to
that time the mass of the people showed complete
indifference to what is now called " vital religion."
Manners were brutish, drunkenness and obscenity
prevailed, but things now began to alter. We
cannot dwell on details, but give one or two extracts
from the " Journal."

> " Friday, April 6th, 1759. We rode over the
> wolds to North Elkington, three miles from
> Louth. The congregation was large, not-
> withstanding the rain, which drove full in
> our face till we came to Grimsby."

(He was preaching also at Scawby, Brigg, Clee-
thorpes, Louth, and Tealby.)

> " June, 1788. Preached in church at Grimsby,
> the Vicar reading prayers (a notable change
> this), not so crowded in the memory of man."

He was then in his eighty-fifth year, and was just
completing fifty years of incessant travelling,
preaching, and administrative labour for the " people
called Methodists." He was nearly seventy when

he first indulged in a carriage on his journeys instead of horseback.

Wherever he went he gained not only adherents but enthusiastic helpers, willing to tramp the country, to preach and to toil. In a crude and elementary way these men followed their master in showing their faith by their works, and in a very practical way faced something little removed from martyrdom as the penalty for their " eccentricities." Hunger and thirst were matters of almost daily experience, hustling and pelting by angry mobs, refusal of lodging or shelter, and constant threats of being " locked up," seem to have been cheerfully encountered. One man (Capiter) is said to have been " tarred and feathered," and more than once " put in the stocks " for preaching.

Wesley's own religious fervour was equalled by his wondrous capacity for work, and his stern determination that his followers should see no flinching in their leader. He is estimated to have covered 250,000 miles in his journeys. He founded several charities on sound and practical bases, he published books, sermons, and pamphlets almost by the score, and as these, increasing in value, brought him some £30,000, he gave it all away.

He was once offered ten guineas to sit for his bust. He misunderstood, and said he would not pay for such a vanity. Then it was explained that *he* was to receive the amount. His answer was, " Do you mean to say you will pay *me* this money ? "

and consented. When he received the guineas he
went through the streets with a friend, giving to this
and that case of distress, and landed at last in a
debtors' prison, where as each pitiful story was
brought before him the rest of his funds rapidly
melted. Asked once by the Commissioner of Taxes
to state the extent of his " plate " for assessment,
he replied, " I have two silver spoons here (London)
and two at Bristol. I shall not buy any more
while so many poor want bread."

His literary works were on logic, languages, the
classics, the history of England, ecclesiastical
history, besides more or less full commentaries on
the Old and New Testament. In his time he held
converse with Indian Chieftains, German Princelings,
and English Royalty (Queen Caroline), besides
meeting and partially influencing celebrities of all
kinds, and for many years he seldom rode for less
than sixty or seventy miles a day. The picture
of the venerable, spare, but still lissom and active
figure, when on his last rounds, and with flowing
grey hair, taking leave of his disciples, is touching
enough, and again recalls St. Paul bidding farewell
to the Elders of Ephesus, and leaving them " sorrow-
ing most of all that they should see his face no more."

The " silver cord " was at length " loosed," and
in the spring of 1791, in his eighty-eighth year, he
lay down to die. In his last hours he tried to write,
but the feeble fingers refused their office. He
lifted his hand and collected his strength to say,

" The best of all is, God is with us," repeating this afterwards in yet stronger tones; then slowly and faintly whispering, " Farewell ! Farewell ! " he passed away.

They laid him in the chapel, and 10,000 men and women passed beside the still form and the worn face, and then they buried him in front of the homely temple he had built in Moorfields, and whose walls he loved as a Jew of old loved Zion. The City Road Chapel has since been the " Mecca " of all sincere Methodists from the uttermost parts of the earth, and has resounded to the voices of Dr. Collyer, Morley Punshon, Jabez Bunting, and all the greater lights of Wesleyan Methodism. Dean Stanley is reported to have stood in the pulpit on one occasion reading aloud some passages of Scripture, and to have said he would " give a great deal " to preach from that spot. It was perhaps on a similar visit that the Dean and the then Home Secretary stood by Wesley's tomb, and the question was asked, " Is this ground consecrated ? " The attendant said, " Yes." " By what Bishop ? " " By holding the body of John Wesley." Then said the Dean, " A very good answer."

They show his clock (of the grandfather species), his bureau, and his big tea-pot, of which he made somewhat extravagant use, but specially his chair, in which every President of Conference has to sit on his inauguration, and it may be noted as a curious instance of the ineradicable hankering of the human mind for relics and memorials (bones of saints, authenticated hair shirts, and the like), that the keys and Bible of the founder of Methodism are handed over to each succeeding President as he takes the chair. One can imagine a time when those keys will be solemnly jingled and that well-worn volume waved to and fro in front of a kneeling congregation of devotees. Such things *have* happened.

This is not the place to discuss, with any fulness, the bearings of Wesley's religious teaching. That he was blamably credulous in accepting shriekings, convulsions, and a sort of midsummer madness of religious ecstacy as " manifestations of the Spirit," must be admitted by all who read of his life and work in an impartial spirit. That he was constantly imposed on by so-called " conversions," resulting in " backsliding," to his own deep disappointment, is equally evident. He was inconsistent in advocating, at one time, vehemently, something as Divine truth, which at another time he either treated with indifference or actively opposed, and he appears to have failed, unmistakably, in drawing the proper sharp line with his female followers, between fatherly or brotherly spiritual counsel and what the irreverent of the present day would call " spooning." No purer man, in his passions and his intentions, probably ever lived, but the stories of Sophia Causton, Sarah Ryan, and others, show that an evangelist is not always and necessarily a man of sense.

THE WORLD IS MY PARISH

S<small>TATUE OF</small> W<small>ESLEY</small>. (In front of City Road Chapel.)

At fifty he decided to marry, after having in previous years written a paper on celibacy, but he had taken godly counsel with his colleagues, and, at least in one quarter, made a previous distinct advance towards matrimony. This latter having failed, he turned to a widow, formerly a domestic servant, with four children and some money, but the money he seems never to have touched. For twenty years this woman made his life, so far as in *her* lay, a misery, by nagging jealousy, prying into his private letters, purloining his loose cash, and, at least on one occasion, pulling his hair out. At length she left him, and he records, tersely enough, "I did not forsake her, I did not dismiss her, I will not recall her." She had a show of religion when he first knew her, and so, for the twentieth time, John Wesley was misled into a belief in some sort of spiritual leading. Some of his biographers are judiciously reticent as to his married relations, but it appears pretty well established that he shared the fate of Socrates with his estimable Xantippe, of the patriarch Job, and that latter-day Job, the late lamented Mr. Caudle. There are traces of the couple travelling together again after the separation, but there is no sign of a lasting or effective reconciliation, and Mrs. Wesley died about nine years after : it is not shown where or how.

We cannot discuss the deep questions of theology and the spirit life which occupied the mind and heart of Wesley for more than half-a-century.

Free-will and predestination, " final perseverance,"
and the doctrine of " perfection," " the witness of
the Spirit," and the frantic sense of " reprobation,"
the non-necessity of Church orders for street and
field preaching, his partnership with Whitefield and
his parting from him, his reports, made in all good
faith, and with the utmost gravity, of the curing of
mad women by prayer, wrestling, and the direct
intervention of the Deity ; his reasons for persisting,
up to the time of his death, in separating men from
women in his chapels, and all the broad and narrow
views which he took up, laid aside, and then was
" guided " to take up again, must simply be mentioned as qualifying, not explaining, his marvellous
personality. *That* stands out above all the din
of sectarian controversy in his time as gigantic
and unquestionable, and the millions all over this
planet whose lives have been influenced for good,
form the " great cloud of witnesses " who vouch for
the tenacity of his faith and the indestructibility
of his work.

Wesleyan Methodism experienced the usual fate,
in one respect, of all new religions or sections of
religion. Quickly after his death came disputes
and secessions, and we now have the original body,
following the exact ideas of the founder, Primitive
Methodists, Bible Christians, Methodist New Connection, United Free Church Methodists, and other
bodies, either here or in the United States.

We are not specially concerned with the historical

accuracy of Thomas Babington, Lord Macaulay,
or the value of his dicta upon other people's work,
literary or otherwise, but it may be just worth
while quoting some words of his on Wesley, as
under :

> "A man whose eloquence and logical acuteness
> might have made him eminent in literature,
> whose genius for government was not inferior
> to that of Richelieu, and who, whatever his
> errors may have been, devoted all his powers
> in defiance of obloquy and derision to what
> he sincerely considered as the highest good
> of his species."—*Essay on "Southey's Col-*
> *loquies on Society."*

CHAPTER XV.

THE GRAFTING OF THE "ROSE OF LANCASTER."

OUR county was the scene of some notable events in the time of Edward IV. That truculent scion of the House of York had, in his loyal adherence to certain maxims, such as "self-preservation the first law of nature," "dead men tell no tales," etc., cut off the head of one Lord Wells, after promising him he should be spared. The son of the slain noble took up arms against the only half-established Monarch, and there must have been some general as well as personal dissatisfaction in the country, as 30,000 men gathered to Sir Robert Wells' standard at Lincoln, and the Knight was enabled to march against the King's troops near Stamford. A great and bloody battle there ensued, but no doubt the half-armed levies of the rebels were no match for the seasoned men in Edward's pay, and who had probably fought in many of the " Red and White " life and death struggles. Wells was defeated, and, with a number of his friends, taken prisoner. They were all put to death by Edward's order, and it would seem that this particular Yorkist must have had a foreshadowing of the Spanish Marshal who, on his death bed, enjoined by his confessor to forgive his enemies, said he could not well do that, as he had shot them all! Ten thousand men are said to have perished on that stricken field, and so frightened were the men of Lincolnshire, and so determinedly did they bolt, that they threw away their coats as they ran, and to such a tune, that the engagement has been ever since known as the " battle of lose coat field." It is a sort of pendant or counterpart to the " Lewis Fair," referred to in a previous chapter, and in which the boot was rather on the other leg.

Edward's life was a short and, in a sense, a merry one. " A man of war from his youth," he was powerfully built, tall, handsome, hardy, and gallant in actual battle, but remorseless to his foes, cruel in the revenge he took upon all opposed to him, as soon as he had them in his power, and steeped to the lips in forfeited oaths and broken promises. Withal gay and courtly in manner, rich and showy in attire, " *bon vivant* " to the last, fighting, carousing, chambering, all came alike to him, and he completed his bustling record at forty-one! He seems to have been popular with nobles and fighting men for his personal bravery and soldierly bearing, and with the trading classes for his open-handedness and the fillips he was always giving to " business " by court entertainments. Poor Henry VI., with his vigils, his counting of beads, his spare living, and his monkish ways, had no chance against the " popular idol " sort of rôle affected by Edward. But the Nemesis we can often see, but not account for, followed the Yorkist King. He or his associates murdered the old King, imprisoned the strenuous Margaret, slew the young Edward their son, the presumptive Prince of Wales, in the very blossom of his young manhood, and ruthlessly took the heads of the best and bravest Lancastrians. The answer came in the mysterious fate, if not the actual murder in the Tower, of his own two boys, the carnage of Bosworth field, and the naked body of his brother and chief helper, Richard of Gloucester, as it was thrown across a horse and hurried to an ignominious grave.

We may notice in passing that Edward was at Stamford in 1462, and was entertained by Alderman John Brown (an uncompromising, straightforward English name !), no doubt on account of the King having lately incorporated the town by letters patent. He was again there in July, 1473, and lodged at the house of the " Friars Minor." He died apparently of " gross living," and was not a King of whom we can be proud.

It was Edward IV. who, in the fifth year of his reign, made Lincoln City, with the townships of Bracebridge, Canwick, Branston, and Waddington, into a county to be called the " Liberty of Lincoln," and two years later gave Grantham its charter, with the right of sending two members to Parliament.

And now we come to Richard, the "wretched, bloody, and usurping boar" of Shakespeare, and Third of the name. Readers are probably too intelligent to require to be told of the controversy as to the real character and appearance of this supposed fiend in human shape ; the efforts to rehabilitate him, the doubts as to his having been the crook'd-back ruffian he has been handed down to us, and the possibility that, after all, he was not so much worse than his contemporaries. That he promptly sliced off the heads of any who stood in his way goes without saying : they all did it. That he connived at, if even he did not order, the murder of the two innocent boys in the Tower, is more than probable. Yorkist and Lancastrian alike had steeped themselves to the chin in the blood of pretty boys, "political" women, and innocent but "inconvenient" nobles of the opposing party. But looking at the almost total destruction of records in the course of the Wars of the Roses, the complete triumph at last of the Tudor-Lancaster faction, the probable suppression of much evidence that might tell in favour of Richard, and the fact that to err is human, and to curry favour with the "powers that be" most particularly human, we must give Richard "a chance." Shakespeare himself may have yielded to the temptation to paint as a monster of iniquity the man who had been the formidable and not unpopular rival of Queen Elizabeth's grandfather, Henry VII. The irascible lady with the uncertain

Tudor temperament, would not have been likely to
" stand any nonsense " with a " play actor fellow "
trying to do justice to one of the toughest, albeit one
of the most unscrupulous, of the House of York.
There is *some* reason to believe that Richard was of
gallant presence ; it is certain that he could fight like
a tiger, was skilful as a general, politic in council, and
reasonably considerate, when he had got the power,
for the interests of the country.   It seems also pretty
clear that he *was* acclaimed at first by the citizens of
London, as, on the whole, the best man for the terrible crisis through which the nation had still to pass,
and it scarcely seems likely that, if his assumption
of power had not been generally condoned, he would
have left the capital, as he did, within a few days of
his accession, for a prolonged tour through some of
the principal towns and country districts.   In the
summer of 1483 he set out from London, and after a
stay at Windsor, passed through Oxford, Warwick,
Tewkesbury, and York, and, as it appears, returning
thence, came to Lincoln.   There he first heard that
Buckingham, a distant cousin of the Royal House,
and who had backed him in all his schemes, was
turning tail and raising forces against him.   It may
be that the Duke had heard of the supposed murder
of the Princes, and considered that deed to have been
" going too far."   Anyhow, the King could not
afford to give away chances, and so immediately
sent round to muster his supporters.   It was at this
time, October 12th, 1483, that he gave orders at Lin-

coln for the apprehension of Buckingham, and, that everything might be done in nice, correct, and proper form (the third Richard no doubt hated irregularity of any kind!) he wrote to the Bishop of Lincoln, who was also Chancellor of the Kingdom at that time, to bring or send the Great Seal, that it might be duly attached to the warrant. There is a "*fac-simile*" of this letter in the British Museum, and after the formal legal wording ("trusty and well beloved," and all that) the writing is alleged to be in Richard's own hand. It is a bold, decided piece of caligraphy, unmistakable in the upness and downness of its strokes, and certainly looks like the writing of a master of men, one who knew his own mind and meant having his own way, or, in default,—"ructions." The gist of the letter is : "Here loved be God, is all well, and truly determined, and to resist the malice of him who had best cause to be true, the Duke of Buckingham, the most untrue creature living, whom, with God's grace, we shall not be long till that we will be in that party's (*those parts*) and subdue his malice. We assure you there was never traitor better purveyed for, as this bearer of Gloucester shall show you."

The last words seem to mean a reproach to Buckingham for his ingratitude for favours conferred by Richard, but that again is "nought," as in those days, even more than now, gratitude was the "sense of favours to come," and favours past were just, in nigger phrase, "no count." The day

before this letter the King had sent another from
Lincoln to the Corporation of York, to meet him
with a " body of horse " for the coming conflict,
and on October 16th the Great Seal was despatched from London by the Bishop and Chancellor,
reaching Richard at Grantham on the 19th. The
result was utter defeat of Buckingham, and the usual
penalty of a missing head, Henry Stafford being
executed at Shrewsbury " without legal process,"
but " by the King's bare order," November
3rd, 1483. There is record of the warrant being
signed by Richard at the Angel Hotel. Our great
poet has drawn a pitiful picture of the Duke on
the road to the block, and it is all very touching
and pathetic, but we may take it that the Duke was
not by any means the lamb-like innocent he is
made to appear in that last sad scene. He had just
played against Richard for well-understood stakes
and lost, that is all.

Buckingham's dying words, as framed by Shakespeare :

> " Lead me to the block of shame,
> Wrong hath but wrong, and blame the due of blame "

and Richard's own frantic and despairing cry at
Bosworth :

> "I have set my life upon a cast,
>   And I will stand the hazard of the die,"

suited master and man alike—gamesters both.

Henry the Seventh proved a wise and competent

King.   Gairdner speaks of him as the " most pacific
Prince that ever reigned." Fatherless from baby-
hood, and delicate in health, he yet became accomplished in languages, skilled in arms, and politic
by nature, taught by the troubles of his youth and
early manhood.   Trained to a general knowledge of
men and things by exile and an enforced sojourn at
foreign courts, he took up the game of diplomacy
abroad and reasonable compromise with faction at
home, as almost a past master in the arts of statesmanship and of leading and ruling men. Com-
plications with the German Emperor Maximilian,
Ferdinand and Isabella of Spain, and James of
Scotland, wars with France, the pretentions of
Pope Alexander the Sixth, the marriage of his
daughter with the Scotch King, and repeated
rebellions engineered by his powerful enemies on
behalf of Lambert Simnel, the reputed son of the
Duke of Clarence and nephew of Richard III., and
also of Perkin Warbeck, alleged to be the Duke of
York, second son of Edward IV., and *not* murdered
in the Tower ; all these found him alert, cool, wary,
and determined, and he seems to have consolidated his power until he became one of the chief
factors to be reckoned with in the ever-seething
cauldron of European politics, and a stalwart and
masterful representative of England's still growing
greatness.

The prophecy of Henry VI. to his council, as he
laid his hands on the head of the boy Earl of

M

Richmond, was amply fulfilled, if the poet may be trusted as also the accurate historian :

> " Come hither, England's hope : If secret powers
> Suggest but truth to my divining thoughts,
> This pretty lad will prove our country's bliss.
> His looks are full of peaceful majesty,
> His head by nature framed to wear a crown,
> His hand to wield a sceptre ; and himself
> Likely in time to bless a regal throne.
> Make much of him, my lords ; for this is he
> Must help you more than you are hurt by me."
>
> SHAKESPEARE : HENRY VI., Loq.

Henry's title, Earl of Richmond, was one of the most ancient in the land, and had been in one branch or other of his family for centuries. They had a seat in the parish of Boston, either early in or prior to the 13th century. His mother, Margaret, Countess of Richmond, was received into the sisterhood of Croyland in 1464, with her mother, the Duchess of Somerset. No doubt this was for safety in those disturbed times. Henry was then but seven years old, and for most of his time in care of one of his uncles.

The Lady Margaret, one of the most illustrious and accomplished women in history, afterwards came into possession of Tattershall Castle, and, still later (1487), was granted by the King, her son, the manor and lands, but there is nothing to show that she ever lived for any time in the castle. Henry's boyhood and early manhood were full of vicissitudes, and his exile in the suspicious atmosphere of Brittany, always liable to be handed over to the relentless Richard as the "Rose of Lancaster," threatening his throne and life, was so precarious as to be only preferable to the still more dangerous air of England. He weathered the breakers, and as the Yorkist King, by his fierce dominance and cruel suppressions, alienated one by one the more powerful nobles of his own faction, they rallied to Henry, and openly or secretly worked for him. At length came the landing at Milford Haven, Bosworth Field, the crowning after the battle, and the proclamation of the new King in the capital.

Amongst other acts of sovereignty he confirmed "all franchises, lands, possessions, rights, and legacies" to the Prior and Convent of Spalding, and it is curious that this took 139 articles to make binding, just 100 more than are necessary for the doctrinal security of the Church of England. The letters patent were upon vellum, under his Great Seal by "*Inspeximus*." It was in the ninth year of his reign that a notable Bishop of Lincoln and Chancellor of the Kingdom, as previously mentioned, John Russell, died at Nettleham, in the Palace, of which there is now no trace, and was buried in the Cathedral. "A learned man, and of great piety and charity." He had been "much esteemed" by King Richard, and was no doubt valued also by Henry. He built the curious chapel on the east of the great south door.

Henry left London (after the proclamation there,

with the usual "rejoicings" and much "junket-
ing "), March, 1486, and rode by way of Cambridge,
Huntingdon, and Stamford to Lincoln, keeping
Easter at the latter city, and "washing the feet of
twenty-nine poor men on Maunday Thursday,"
for the very sufficing reason that he was then
twenty-nine years old. He went on further, but
shortly summoned a number of the men of Lincolnshire to meet him to oppose one of the frequent
rebellions that beset his reign. Later, he again
visited the city after defeating one of the Lambert
Simnel combinations, and relegating that interesting
youth to the position of scullion in the Royal
kitchen. It is noticeable that while Edward IV.
and others conducted the butchery business on
wholesale lines, and it may be added " for exporta-
tion," as when he didn't cut off the heads of his
enemies he exiled them, Henry leant rather to the
retail branch, and killed only a limited number
under a supposed dire necessity, putting the rest of
his foes, on this occasion, under lock and key, or
fining them handsomely all round.

Some histories show that Henry went almost
straight to Lincoln from Bosworth, and *there* was
crowned in his camp, and spent three days in processions and stately ceremonials, public prayers
and thanksgivings being offered for the "signal
victory." As, however, there is little doubt that
he had assumed all the prerogatives of kingship on
the battlefield, and had had Richard's crown placed

on his head, and, as his own claim was not unassailable, it is probable that he contented himself with the power without bothering himself too much about the prescriptive forms. Thenceforward he not only reigned but governed, and much of the legislation of the time was due to his personal initiative and strong will. He has the reputation of being the best of England's lawgiving Kings next to Edward I. He reformed the currency (and made money by it), but kept up a reserve fund, not for any special luxuries of his own, but to meet foreign wars and home disturbances ; he regulated the administration of Justice, did his best to support commerce and manufactures, worked at the checking of depopulation sometimes going on, encouraged English shipping, forbade payment in gold to foreigners, and in many ways, not legitimate perhaps now, but according to his then lights, strove to build up the prosperity of his country. Grave in his bearing, stately in intercourse with nobles or citizens, maintaining well the dignity of a powerful sovereign, he was yet suave, kindly, and, on occasion, pleasantly humorous. He had his aberrations. For reasons of state, after the death of his Queen, Elizabeth of York, he tried to marry his own daughter-in-law, Catherine, widow of his eldest son Arthur, who had died early, and, this failing, he actually essayed to wed that lady's sister, Juana of Castile, known to be out of her mind. But the cloudy times and the necessity for steering the nation through many a crisis must weigh in his favour. He died a widower at fifty-two (1509), and left £18,000,000 in cash and securities as a nice little capital for his second son, Henry VIII., to commence business with.

In this reign, one William Rennington, son of Robert Rennington, fishmonger, of Boston, was Lord Mayor of London (1500), and there was born at Grantham Richard Fox, afterwards Bishop of Winchester.

An interesting incident also, for Lincolnshire, is the passage through the county, in 1502, of Henry's daughter, Margaret, betrothed to James IV. of Scotland, from which union sprang the Stuart dynasty. Henry accompanied the Princess to Northampton, and there took leave of her. She rode through Stamford to Grantham, escorted by the Earl of Surrey and a great company of nobles, and we transcribe from an old record the fine doings at that place :

"About foure myles from Grauntham, the Alderman, accompanied with the Bourgesses and inhabitants of Grauntham, in fayre Order, receyved hyr to the number of four score horses hounestly appoynted, and conveyed hir to the towne.

"Without the said towne was the processyon in fayre order, the colledge of the said place and Freres Mendicants, the wich receyved hyr in synging Laudes. And att the sayd place lightyd of his horse my lord the Bishop of Norwich ; the wich gaff her the crossys for to kysse—and thus was doon continually, lasting the sayd veyage thorough the Reyme of Englaunde in all the places wher she cam.

"This doon she was brought with the sayd Compayne in fayre aray to hyr lodgings, that was with a Gentylman called Mr. Hioll.

"Through all the goode townes and villages where she past, all the Bells wer rong dayly. And by the way cam the habitants of the countrey for to see the noble company, bryngyng greate vessels full of Drynk, and gyffing the same to them that nedde had of it, saying, that if better they had had, better they should have brought.

"The next day after, being Sounday, the 9th day of the monneth of Jully, she abode all the day in the sayde town of Grauntham.

"The Xth day of the sayd month, the sayd Quene departed from Grauntham hyr company in fayre order and the sayd Alderman and with him the Bourgesses and Habitants conveyed hyr by the space of 3 miles, and then took ther Lycence.

"A myle from Grauntham was semled the company of the Sheryf of the Countye of Lincoln, well drest, all on horseback, to the number of XXX horses, the wich were presented by the sayd Robert Dymock to the said Quene for to do hyr service and conveyde hyr to Newerke."

CHAPTER XVI.

A Soul's Shipwreck. (Dr. Dodd, LL.D.)

WE must now have a change. It is not good for
Lincolnshire folk to have a too high opinion of
themselves, *qua* Lincolnshire. It would be regret-
table to notice some worthy Bostonian crossing his
market-place on inch-and-a-half heels, and with head
erect, murmuring to himself, " I thank the goodness
and the grace," " I was not born as thousands are,"
and so on, or a Town Councillor of Lincoln, striding
with tip-tilted nose beneath the Stonebow, and
thinking out a paraphrase of old Job's words, "No
doubt *we* are the people, and wisdom (to say nothing
of learning, poetry, gallantry in arms, and a few
other things) shall die with us." We have " en-
thused " just a little too much. We are showing
the sturdy fighter and grand explorer and discoverer,
one of the greatest scientists of the ages, a poet of
first rank, an Archbishop of the English Church,
and a divine of world-wide celebrity and success, all
Lincolnshire born. We are in danger of reversing
the inquiry of Nathanael, and of being driven to ask
"*Can* anything evil have come out of such a county?"

So, in medical parlance, we will supply a gentle
" alterative " by glancing at one who had to end
a curious career at Tyburn Tree.

But what about consistency ? Why class *him*
as one of our " worthies ? " Well, in the first place,
life is a poor tame thing without an occasional
inconsistency, and in the next place he *was* worthy of
—more than a passing notice. The reader will
forgive us. We are no mere sensation-mongers,
and we are not going to defile these pages with
scribblings of the " Newgate Calendar " order, but
there are points in this life to which we may well
give heed, and of which it may be retorted to the
Pharisee, with his " Pooh ! the fellow was hung at
Tyburn ! "—" Who art thou that judgest another ? "
and, " Let him that thinketh he standeth take
heed lest *he* fall."

William Dodd was born in 1729 at Bourne.
There seems no ignoring the record that he *was*
a Lincolnshire man. One soul planet issuing from
the mysterious void, one knows not why, to whirl
through a confused and treacherous orbit of London
life, of " fal, lal " society and laced handkerchief
religion, to find its perihelion as a sort of court
chaplain to fine ladies troubled with the " vapours "
and swells in search of a sensation : then wandering
from its centre of gravity to collapse in darkness
and ruin at the gallows. His father was the Vicar,
and must have done his best with the boy, for he
grew up well informed, if not learned, facile of

speech and prolific of pen work. A whole library of sermons, essays, controversial tracts and pamphlets, and even poems (of a sort) attest at least his activity of mind and body, a certain amount of accomplishment and a certain (or uncertain?) determination to find a sphere and to fill it decently. He projected and partly carried out, though it is admitted with much secretarial help of others, a comprehensive commentary on the Bible, he essayed to write in Latin as well as English, and to this day Dodd's " Beauties of Shakespeare " is referred to by many who havn't an idea as to who " Dodd " was, or that his end was with a rope.

There is little to say of his boyhood. His family would not probably have cared to supply details, but preferred that his memory should be sheltered, so far as might be, by a friendly oblivion. At sixteen he went to Cambridge, matriculated the next year, and took his degree three years later (1749). Even in those young days he wrote of things serious and comic, mostly in the flippant and foolish strain. He did worse than write them, he *printed* them, and afterwards, like the typical dog returning to his vomit, he collected and republished these doubtful productions of a questionable wit. He began to ape the " swell " man of genius. A sort of " tuppenny " Horace Walpole, he took to expensive dress and surroundings, danced and frivolled generally, and so at twenty went to London to seek fame and fortune in literary circles. The

innate levity of his nature led him to plunge into
gayeties of any kind. It seems about this time
that he wrote a comedy, which he was obliged by
the authorities to withdraw from publication or
performance, and having, we may suppose, come
to the conclusion that his " *métier* " was the salvation of human souls through the ministry of the
Church, he took orders, and was appointed to the
curacy of " West Ham," then a quiet rural village,
but for *him*, fatally near London. He had married
one Mistress Mary Perkins, a not very high-born
daughter of a poor Durham Prebendary, and whatever may be said as to the women being at the
bottom of every mischief in connection with the
wide race of man, there is nothing to show that this
attachment was not a perfectly honest and genuine
one on both sides.

For a time Dodd seems to have had a dream
of rural and domestic felicity, plus spiritual
progress and usefulness, but it was only a dream.
" The common round, the daily toil," were not
for him, and in the intervals of pastoral visits
and administering the Sacraments, he wrote a
novel, which can only be termed *risqué*. It is
singular that in this book he leads his villain to the
gibbet, paints for us gruesome pictures of the life
in Newgate, and altogether seems under some sort of
spell of morbid fascination for the criminal and
immoral side of things. Indeed, in most of what
he wrote there ran a strain of pruriency, inborn,

perhaps, but nourished and developed by the fœtid atmosphere in which his French-polished rakes and his women of " *ton* " smirked and gallivanted and scribbled bad verses. He, no doubt, made an honest effort to fill his position of Parish Priest, at least with decency and some amount of effectiveness, and long after, in his hour of trial and in the very shadow of death, his backward glance upon this period of his life found expression in the smooth, velveteeny, milk-and-water lines for which he was so incorrigible :

> " Return blest hour, ye peaceful days return !
> When through each office of celestial love,
> Ennobling piety my glad feet led
> Continual, and my head each night to rest
> Lull'd on the downy pillow of content !
> Dear were thy shades, O Ham ! and dear the hours
> In manly musing 'midst thy forests pass'd
> And antique woods of sober solitude,
> O Epping ! witness to my lonely walks."

Poor simpering, sentimental, philandering, and invertebrate Dodd ! A little more self-control, and less self-consciousness, a few pounds more of " ballast," and he might not have committed forgery or perpetrated such " poetry." He had seen Garrick play, and had mixed a good deal with much of the literary and dramatic talent of the day, though not probably of the calibre either of that great artist or of Sheridan or Edmund Burke. He had acquired a sugary, mincing eloquence, his sermons seem to have been stuffed with shoddy

WILLIAM DODD, LL D.

[Mr. J. F. De

sentiment and pinchbeck imagery.   He could write
a poem on "Lady Hertford in tears," and could
criticise Laurence Sterne for writing "Tristram
Shandy," thus (1765 ?) :

> " Is it for this you wear the sacred gown ?
>
>   * * * *
>
> Is it for this the sacred page was given
> To teach high truths and point the way to heaven ? "

There is little doubt that he persuaded himself
at times that he really was a gifted messenger on
Divine things, if not to the great vulgar herd of
mankind, at least to those lost sheep whose ways
were so particularly like those of the goat, and who
dangled through what was then called "Society."
So he was ripe in character and accomplishments
for the appointment which led by sure steps to his
moral and material overthrow.   He associated
himself with some of his swell friends in founding
the "Magdalene Institution" for women of a certain
class, and he was made chaplain !   In this post he
soon became the vogue (1761-3).   Fashion and rank
went to listen to his sweet sermons, in which he
could so ably blend piquant allusion to sin with a
saintly inculcation of that charity which " covereth
a multitude," and, of course, the particular one then
in question.   The fair penitents in the front row
and a "fetching" uniform often wept at the remembrance of their frailty, and the high ladies in
the audience dusted their eyes with elegant " *mou-
choirs*," and had—similar ideas.   Everybody who

(jaded by disposition and "*blasé*" with things in general) wanted something titivating, foregathered at the "Magdalene," including a Royal Prince and lots of the aristocracy, and they must have derived much comfort from the reflection that, after all, vice was not so very vicious, "debauchery" might reasonably be altered to some less offensive term, and that, as there is a "good deal of human nature in man" (and woman) we must be careful to make generous allowances. And then the collections were so satisfactory ! It is stated that on one occasion the Magdalene sermon brought near £1,400, whilst Sterne, preaching for the Foundling Hospital, could only draw £400.

The Doctor now went "full steam ahead." Some of his friends got him made Royal Chaplain (at thirty-three !), he introduced himself by one of his inevitable sonnets to the Bishop of St. David's, and *he* gave him a prebend. A windfall came to Mrs. Dodd from a relative, and this he devoted to acquiring a chapel of ease of his own in Pimlico, which he named the "Charlotte," after the Queen ; he became tutor to Lord Chesterfield's son, who afterwards gave evidence in court helping to convict him of the capital crime ; he had rooms as chaplain in the Royal Palace, and went partners in a second chapel in Bloomsbury with a fellow clergyman. We see him thus on the flood-tide of success, with his gay little flutterings in the "world of fashion," his City dinners, his West End tea drinkings, his crowded congregations, his rustling silk gown and full-bottomed wig, his coach, his "book of poems," his ceaseless stream of lisping verse, his editing of the *Christian Magazine*, his debts, and the "annuities" he had been raising to meet his extravagant outlay.

Dodd had tried his best to get into the famous "Literary Club," but the attempt met with "cold obstruction." Dr. Johnson himself said afterwards, "It would not have done that one of our club should have been hanged," "not but" (cheerfully) "that some of them deserved it." He had been to Cambridge (1766) again and taken his degree as LL.D., and so far as outward show and a sublime indifference to any need for harmonising preaching with practice could carry him, he was a successful man, envied and courted, but always in debt, always struggling to maintain an "establishment" with limited means, always "cadging" for further preferments of some better value in money than those he held, so that he might have the wherewith to "keep the pot a-boiling," and to steady his feet in the perilous game of "see-saw" he played for years.

He managed to get presented to a rectory and vicarage, in addition to the appointments he already held, but there was not much pay attached to them, and the life of "bluff," false glitter, and shifty finance had to go on. Shakespeare's Wolsey, in his fall, exclaims—

" I have ventured
Like little wanton boys who swim on bladders,
These many summers in a sea of glory.
But, far beyond my depth, my high-blown pride
At length broke under me, and now has left me,
Weary and old with service, to the mercy
Of a rude stream that must for ever hide me."

Dodd was not a Wolsey, and he wasn't "old" when his doom came, but he must have been "weary" of smirking hypocrisy and all but blasphemous exploiting of the religious sentiment for his personal advantage.

And now, in 1774, he was "hard up." His wife (no doubt the Doctor knew all about it, if even he did not instigate her action) wrote privately to the wife of the Lord Chancellor offering a heavy bribe, or benefices of considerable value, in exchange, providing that the living of St. George's, Hanover Square, then vacant, and with a stipend of £1,500 a year, could be secured for him. The lady showed the letter to the great man, and Dodd was dismissed his Royal Chaplaincy, although many believed his story that he had known nothing of his wife's indiscretion, and that he attributed her action to a loveable, but unwise, zeal for his welfare. Society was divided into those who still believed in the man, or at least thought he and his wife were "no worse than others," and those who now openly jeered at the "Macaroni Doctor," and clamoured at his pretensions.

" *Facilis descensus Averni*," and the road downward was in this case more than usually slippery. He had been glorified in the public prints thus : " Yesterday the Rev. Dr. Dodd preached before their Majesties and their Royal Highnesses the Dukes of Gloucester and Cumberland, at the Chapel Royal, St. James'. The Sword of State was carried to and from chapel by the Right Hon. Lord Cadogan.

" On Monday the Rev. Dr. Dodd had the honour to present to His Royal Highness the Prince of Wales a volume of sermons on the ' Duties of the Great,' which their Majesties have permitted him to dedicate to the Prince, and which were most graciously received."

The little Prince, of eight or ten, and who afterwards developed into that most revered monarch George IV., must have wept tears of gratitude during his blameless young manhood and high-souled maturity as he thought of the devoted mentor of his childhood dressing his affectionate counsels in these eloquent and silvery periods. We all know how he *profited* by them.

The game was up, and this poor shambling exemplar of the " Pilgrim's Progress " was nearing the " Slough of Despond," from which there should be no " Mr. Help " strong enough to lift him, and was to pass through a "Valley of Humiliation" and a combat with an Apollyon which should be no glorious allegory of an " inspired tinker," but an awful, cruel reality of experience almost unique in our records. He went to the Continent for a time, apparently to

N

" let the storm blow over," and even there could not keep out of the " vain world." He returned, and, pressed, as ever, for ready money, his borrowing powers exhausted, like those of a modern limited company, at his wits' end and desperate, he wrote in the signature of his quondam pupil, Stanhope, now Lord Chesterfield, to a bond for £4,200. This was a much larger sum than he really wanted, but more likely to pass with little question than a smaller amount, which in the case of so great a noble would have seemed paltry, and perhaps have aroused suspicion. The money was got through a banker, and only by the merest fluke was the latter, or a lawyer, led to mention the matter to the Earl, when of course, the bond was denounced and all came out.

The story of Dodd's behaviour on the disclosure is pathetic indeed. His tears, his frantic attempts to convince Lord Chesterfield and his own friends that he meant no harm, that the money would in a brief time have been replaced and the bond quietly destroyed ; that he wouldn't have really robbed the Earl on any account, and that, after all, the *intent* to defraud constituted the criminality, and not the mere writing on a piece of paper of another person's name. All no use ! " Society," that marvellous compound of the " unco' guid," the honest and the well meaning, the humbug and the charlatan, the swindling trader and the sharp practitioner who quietly does everybody all round but keeps within the law, required an " ex-

ample," or shall we say a—scapegoat ! There had
been some bad cases lately. "Society" must be
protected, the "law" must be "vindicated;"
besides, what a piquant thing it would be for a
Doctor of Laws and a great theological authority to
swing for forgery, and "what a day we could have
out there at Tyburn !"

So, to his increasing horror, the Doctor found
himself before the Lord Mayor and afterwards at the
Old Bailey, many of his friends doubting and dis-
trusting, the Earl cold and indifferent, his numerous
enemies exultant and triumphant, and he himself
shivering with apprehension as one by one each
loophole of escape was stopped, each miserable
technical plea overruled, and the dreadful octopus
fangs of the law fastened themselves in his trembling
personality. But he never, till the last, seems to
have dreaded the worst. At once, on discovery of
the forgery, he had refunded the greater part of the
money to the banker defrauded, and *this money
was accepted*, with an undertaking from him for a
few hundreds of balance. Punishment, yes ! Loss
of position, abject humiliation, perhaps ? imprison-
ment ? transportation ? But, oh ! not—no ! no !
not—the gallows !

It is authentically stated that after his sentence,
and on the very day on which the Governor of the
gaol had informed him of the arrival of the formal
order for his execution, he handed to the Editor of
the *Morning Chronicle* a "comedy," and begged his

interest with certain managers to get it brought out !
His friend was shocked, and naturally tried to divert
his mind to more serious thoughts, but Dodd more
than once turned the conversation with " Oh, they
will never hang me ! "

But they did. In spite of the pitiful spectacle
he presented as he fell fainting on the floor of the
dock when sentenced, in spite of his own passionate
cry for mercy to the King, Lord North, and Earl
Mansfield, in spite of powerful influences moving in
his favour, a dignified and logical appeal from Dr.
Johnson, a formal petition from the Common
Council of London, and testimony from many sources
(one memorial was signed by 23,000 people) as to
the good effect by his public ministry, the savage
law of that day was allowed to take its course, the
Press being dead against him, and the " commercial
classes." angrily insistent for an " example."

He preached a sermon (said to have been composed
or suggested by Dr. Johnson) to his fellow-prisoners
in Newgate from the words of David, " I acknow-
ledge my transgression, and my sin is ever before
me." He was visited in prison by John Wesley
(and a strange meeting *that* must have been), he
endured the bitterness of parting with his poor
faithful, crushed, and hysterical wife, and yet he
kept up quite a correspondence with his friends and
acquaintances from his cell, and in the interval
between sentence and death wrote " Thoughts in
Prison," in blank verse and rhyme, 232 pages of

small 8vo print! In that little book the curious in such matters can note the sort of maudlin special pleading which can issue from a condemned cell, and can judge for themselves how far unblushing hypocrisy or a twisted moral sense are really in the ascendant.

As he slowly realised that hope and human mercy had alike hidden themselves behind the inky cloud of his coming doom, he seems to have braced himself to some measure of manly fortitude, and for the last day or two of life to have put on at least the semblance of Christian resignation, or what he, perhaps, mistook for it, stoical endurance. He was mocked with the luxury of a coach in which to ride to Tyburn, a common highwayman who was to be " removed " at the same time and place being accommodated in the usual cart. Such it was in those days to be esteemed " one of the quality "! He died with some appearance of dignified composure, and we may say of him that " nothing in life became him like the leaving it."

It was a hard, cruel age. Horace Walpole, fine gentleman and champion letter writer of the age, penned scathing words about the poor fallen preacher; the great George Fox and the Abbé Raynal, a Frenchman of note, looked down from a window on the last gruesome scene; West End "sparks" and coffee-house wits rode out to see the show, and the hideous crowd of hanging sightseers was there in all its hellish revelry.

But what would you ? It might have been still
worse had our modern halfpenny newspaper man
been there, with his feverish glance upon every
twitch of the wretched culprit's face, his fingers
shaking with excitement, dotting down every sob
in a teeming note-book, and anxiously watching from
the corners of his eyes that some esteemed Press-
brother should not have " the pull " of him for the
first afternoon edition. " We have progressed since
then ? " Yes—but on the surface or in deed and
in truth ? There are still silk hats and frock coats,
also laces and furbelows, to be seen at the Old Bailey
when a fellow-creature is to be tried for his or her
life, and at the Divorce Court, where one can enjoy a
quiet chuckle at something " racy." We know at
what awesome pace our material world spins itself
round daily, and rolls through the fields of space.
In the moral world we take things quietly, and do
not seek to rival the " music of the spheres " with
any but the slowest of " adagio " movements.

CHAPTER XVII.

WHAT IT IS TO BE " BLUFF."—HENRY VIII.

A STRIKING contrast to the cool, scheming, statesmanlike Henry VII. was his young heir and successor,
" bluff " King Hal.   No doubt, after the turmoil
and blood-letting of the "Roses," there was need
for another masterful and yet wary monarch who
should soothe animosities and " ride the whirlwind "
of Papal and Protestant conflict until *that* storm
should at least partially expend itself.   Whether
he " filled the bill " in this respect every reader
must judge for himself.   A throned monarch at
eighteen, and, like David of old, a " youth ruddy of
countenance " and well favoured ; like Saul, of
stature above his fellows, skilled in all manly exer-
cises, and of some considerable culture in letters,
he seemed indeed to have the world at his feet, but
early developed a " temper," and showed his
" bluffness " mainly in his peculiar treatment of
courtiers, statesmen, personal friends, and—*wives*.
Had he lived in these our days, and had his abode
in Whitechapel, he would have come under the
notice of the police as a licentious scamp, and would

have inevitably " done time " for brutal assaults on the wives of his manly bosom, whether lawfully wedded or not, but being born in the purple and, as we are told, of " the most kingly dignity," he was merely " bluff King Hal," and bullied his statesmen and swore at his " minions " in an exemplary and most Royal manner, to say nothing of taking off the heads of two of his six wives with every polite and genteel accessory of headsman, well-sharpened axe, nice convenient wooden block, guards, a few staring officials, and a respectable Bishop, or other ecclesiastic, to read the final prayers. What could a wife who was " done with," and whose continued presence interfered with one's natural lust for another woman, want more ? Of the two he put away, one probably broke her heart, or at any rate died in loneliness, and another was so ugly as to have shocked the æsthetic sense of this sexagonally married person, and he seems actually to have taken her only on condition that he should immediately divorce her ! No. 6, Catherine Parr, was the only one of these wretched women who may be said to have been above " par," for she decided to survive her Royal husband, and she did. He must have had an uneasy feeling in his last days as he thought of her " living on," neither divorced nor decapitated. The sense of lost opportunities is apt to haunt the remissful monarch as well as any conscience-stricken humbler mortal. But Catherine Parr had been twice married before her promotion

to the Throne. Henry never had the advantage of
the advice of the sententious Mr. Weller, senior,
to "beware of widders!" For No. 3 on the
gruesome list, Jane Seymour, we can only refer to
the dark suspicions current after her death in
childbirth, that her life had been sacrificed to ensure
that of the sickly boy, afterwards Edward VI., and
to satisfy Henry's passionate longing for a male
heir. Anyhow, the "rejoicings" for the birth of
an heir were allowed, with beatings of drums and
braying of trumpets, to disturb the last moments of
the dying Queen.

All this, however, is merely introductory to the
fact that Henry comes rather specifically into the
history of our county. His minister, Thomas
Cromwell, in carrying out reformatory ideas with
what was meant to be judicious moderation, got an
Act passed to enforce the reading of the Lord's
Prayer, the Creed, and the Ten Commandments in
English. This so offended the common people that
they rose (1536) in various places to protest with
vigour against the innovation. Lincolnshire distinguished itself by the first movement, and by an
assembly, we won't say an army, of 20,000 men,
headed by one Captain Cobler, said to have
been really Dr. Mackerel, Abbot of Barlings, a
small village some six miles east of Lincoln, and the
importance of the demonstration may be gathered
from the fact that the King prepared to march
against them in person. There is the usual allega-

tion that the rumpus was worked up by the Latinist
priesthood, and, no doubt, as the shire was early
covered with fine church architecture, patent to the
present day, and many abbeys and monastic houses,
so often the friends of the rustics, there *was* a
feeling of gratitude for past favours and for those
which might yet be " to come." Anyhow, the so-
called insurrection fizzled out, for, on learning of
the King's preparations to meet them, the rebels
sent to him their submission, laid down their arms,
were graciously spoken to by Henry himself, and
got off with some fines upon certain towns, Lincoln
being mulcted in £40. It seems to have been on
this occasion that the " bluff " one gave Lincolnshire an unusually large-sized piece of his mind,
viz., that it was " the most brute and beastalye
county in the Realme." The county did not,
probably, take this as in any way personally offensive. It was, no doubt, a reminiscence in the
King's mind of a similar disturbance, though not
on the same grounds, in Edward the Fourth's time
(See page 170). The £40 would, no doubt, go some
way to soothe the ruffled feelings of the Monarch,
accompanied as it was by £20 from Stamford, £50
from Boston (they must have been *very* naughty
there), the parts of Lindsey £300, and Kesteven
£50. Many religious houses were suppressed in
and about Boston, but Henry afterwards made some
amends to the town by constituting it a " free
Borough " (1546). Mackerel, with the Vicar of

Louth and others, was, however, tried for treason, convicted, and executed at Tyburn (1537).

In 1538 one William Forman, native of Gainsboro', was Lord Mayor of London. There was also born in this reign (1532) Richard Sutton, soldier, merchant, and philanthropist, who founded the Charterhouse School of London, and died 1611. Gainsboro', or a small adjacent village, claims him.

Only at intervals of years did Henry VIII. pass through Stamford (1532, 1539, etc.) and other Lincolnshire towns on his way to and from the North. The " progress " of 1541 was one of the most noteworthy, as affecting Henry's marital relations, for it was then, and at Lincoln, that the lewdness of his fifth wife, Catherine Howard, became apparent, and her guilty relations with one Culpeper in that town was considered to have been proved. She and the Catholic party, however, maintained that the man was but her cousin, trying to make capital out of his relationship. But she confessed, in a general way, before her death to much early looseness, and her case is, no doubt, a worse one than that of the vain and volatile, but not provably *guilty*, Anne Boleyn. A " Norfolk Howard " in a very complete sense, niece of the Duke of that time, young, beautiful, but dissolute, exploited by her uncle in the interest of the Catholic faction, then struggling desperately to maintain its old supremacy, we can only pity the unhappy Catherine, who was tried and condemned with quite unreason-

able promptitude, and not even heard in her own
defence, and lost her pretty head on Tower Hill one
cold grey morning in February, 1542. Of course a
King could have six wives, lawful and unlawful,
and any desirable number of paramours, but a
Queen Consort to compromise her lord's dignity by
sexual looseness—faugh! Curiously enough, two
of the scenes of the wretched little drama embracing
Catherine's "liaisons" were laid in the Bishop's
palace at Lincoln and the "Old Hall" at Gainsboro'.

The Queen confessed to Dr. Longland, Bishop of
Lincoln, her frailty in early youth, apparently the
natural result of a "bad bringing up," but vowed
to the last that she had mended her ways as she
had grown older and wiser, and that, as a wife, she
had been perfectly faithful to Henry.

It was in 1541 that the King and Queen, with a
great retinue, crossed from Hull to Barrow, and
were splendidly entertained by the monks of Thorn-
ton Abbey. He gave them certain special considera-
tions for this at the "dissolution." Then the Royal
pair (there are traces of their being at Grimsby *en
route*) came on to Lincoln, and poor Kate drew near
her doom. The King changed his raiment outside
the city from green velvet to cloth of gold, and the
Queen from crimson velvet to cloth of silver. There
was a grand procession to the Cathedral, with the
usual shouting and clamorous joy-bells, the Bishop
coming out to give the King and Queen the crucifix
to kiss (he was Defender of the Faith, you know),

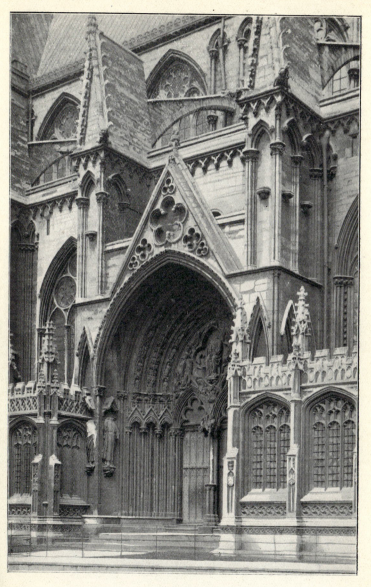

LINCOLN CATHEDRAL. (South Porch.)

HARRISON BROTHERS,]   [*Lincoln*

" T'hole queere (the whole choir) synging melo-
dyouslye ' Te Deu.' " Then the couple went
" vendre ye canaope to the sacrement," and—said
prayers. After that we read instructively, " Itm,
the Mr. of the King's horsse toke the carpetts and
stooles for his ffee." " Itm, the fotemen toke the
canape for *theyre* ffee." Funnily enough, that is
the way this kind of thing is done even down to this
present.

It is difficult, however, to raise the poorest of
smiles when we remember that the unhappy Catherine was then in the hands of blackmailers who knew
her past, that she probably was forced to grant an
interview that very night to one of her old paramours, and that in two or three months after all this
pageantry her headless body was flung into a
dishonoured grave.

The " bluff " King used up his statesmen much
as he used up his wives. Without going into their
moral characteristics, but simply dealing with them
as statesmen, think of three men like Wolsey, Sir
Thomas More, and Sir Thomas Cromwell being
brought to the dust in one passionate, unscrupulous,
self-centred reign, one to die a broken, ruined old
man, the two others to complete a life-long service,
faithful according to their lights, by the usual
" capitation fee " on Tower Hill !

What's the use of indulging in further caustic
comments on " the most religious and gracious
King," Henry ? " Least said soonest mended."

He died at fifty-six, after a reign of thirty-eight
years, dreaded, we need not say hated, to the last,
and yet extracting from his subjects a certain rude
admiration, as for some strong, fierce animal.
Coarse and bloated no doubt in form, by his in-
dulgences, but we may hope not quite a second
Herod.

Lincolnshire does not, probably, feel its soil
especially sanctified by having on several occasions
been trodden by this particular " vicegerent " of
God on earth. We do not know that, in morals,
he was any worse than Francis of France, or several
of the other monarchs of the time, though for sheer
hardness and brutal indifference to the sufferings
of others he would, perhaps, bear away the palm ;
but he *did* make a stiff fight with the Pope, he put
through some difficult work in the shape of wars
with France and the league with Germany, he
posed bravely on the Field of the Cloth of Gold,
and he put Scottish difficulties to rest for a considerable time by the victory of Flodden.

One of the darkest incidents in this reign was the
fate of Anne Ascough (Askew ?), a well-born woman
of South Kelsey, near Caistor. The victim of an
unhappy marriage, forced upon her by her father,
she obtained a divorce from her husband and came
to Court as one of the ladies of Queen Catherine
Parr. There the Romish intriguers, ever at work
to ruin the Queen with Henry, fixed upon Anne and
her reforming tendencies as evidence against her

mistress. She was brought before the Council, condemned, barbarously tortured, and finally burnt with three others in Smithfield. Unable to stand, she was held up by the chain fastening her to the stake, and, being, at the last dread moment, offered pardon on full recantation, refused, crying, " I came not here to deny my Lord," and so died. A true Lincolnshire (and English) lady !

CHAPTER XVIII.

SIR JOHN FRANKLIN.

NOT least on the scroll of famous Englishmen was
that baby boy destined to be, who first saw the
light in 1786 at one of the remote villages of our
county. As a growing lad, probably while located
at Louth Grammar School, he is known to have
looked out from our prosaic coast over the " en-
circling sea " that guards these islands, and from
those early days to have indulged a passion for
penetrating its secrets and exploring its further-
most wastes which never left him till life itself
was spent, and his gallant spirit shook off its weary
tenement of clay' on the shores of King William's
Island. Before that day should come Franklin
had a great deal to " get in." His very name
suggests the sturdy, indomitable Saxon—" Franklin"
being simply " Freeholder " of the times of Cedric,
Godwin, and Harold. He was the youngest of a
family of twelve, most of them notable in some
way. They came of a good stock, as the family
had held up their heads for generations in our
county as " Yeomen," another name for the same

STATUE OF FRANKLIN. (In Spilsby Market Place.)

thing as "Franklin." The elder brother, though a home-keeping man and succeeding his father in "business," managed to raise a troop of cavalry in the war times, and acted as its adjutant. Another brother carried off honours at Oxford, and ended as an Indian Judge; yet again another was major in the East Indian service. John had been destined for the Church, but that walk with a schoolmate from the Louth School to the sea shore, and the outlook over only a corner of Old Neptune's wide domains, seems to have stirred his imagination and fixed his career. He was "for sea" from thence on, and the kindly intent of his father to break the boy's purpose by sending him to Lisbon on a trader, and giving him a rough taste of a "Life on the Ocean Wave," failed of its object. Young John persisted, and the father gave way.

Midshipman on the *Polyphemus*, in 1800, the boy of fourteen took part in the battle of Copenhagen in 1801, his ship leading the attack. Then in the *Investigator*, with Flinders, an able and kindly commander, he sailed the southern seas and rounded Australia, suffering shipwreck on a reef of that little-known coast, and had his first experience of camp life on a sand bank 180 miles from shore, and 750 from any effective help. After that he was with Nelson at Trafalgar as signal midshipman in the *Bellerophon*. Many around him were wounded or killed, but he came off, spared to serve with Cornwallis and St. Vincent, and for six years in the

o

Bedford, on the coasts of Portugal and Brazil and at the siege of Flushing. We find him recorded as wounded in the attack on New Orleans, during which, however, he captured one of the enemy's gunboats.

All this was merely his apprenticeship, and it was not till the mature age of thirty-one that he received his first independent command, and commissioned the modest *Trent*, as consort to the *Dorothea*, on a mandate from the Government to discover a North-West Passage to the shores of India and the glories of the East. He had already traversed parts of that dismal northern region as a subaltern in the " Buchan and Ross " expedition, which returned unsuccessful, and in which the famous Parry had been a fellow " sub." The new attempt (1818) was committed to Franklin and Parry jointly, the two to go different routes and with separate commands ; to meet as might be practicable. Parry achieved almost full success, but " 'Tis not in mortals to *command* success," and John Franklin's daring steps across those silent and eternal wastes were dogged by treachery of Indians, Canadian guides, and Esquimaux ; by losses of provisions vitally necessary for the adventurers, and by a persistent series of smaller or larger obstacles, for which there is no other name than sheer ill fortune.

We catch a partial, but vivid, glimpse of the effect of these in Dr. Richardson's narrative of his arrival at Fort Enterprise, after an enforced separation from his chief during the journey to and from the Coppermine River: "We came in sight of the fort at dusk, and it is impossible to describe our sensations when, on attaining the eminence that overlooks it, we beheld the smoke issuing from one of the chimneys. From not having met with any footsteps in the snow, as we drew nigh our once cheerful residence, we had been agitated by many melancholy forebodings. Upon entering the now desolate building we had the satisfaction of embracing Captain Franklin, but no words can convey an idea of the filth and wretchedness that met our eyes on looking around. Our own misery had stolen upon us by degrees, and we were accustomed to the contemplation of each other's emaciated figures, but the ghastly countenances, dilated eyeballs, and sepulchral voices of Mr. Franklin and those with him were more than we could at first bear."

Such was the result of long months of plodding over frozen solitudes, crossing, and occasional immersion in, ice-bound rivers, feeding on "*tripe de roche*," a lichen of glutinous nature scraped from the rocks, camping at night in wet and frozen clothes, arguing or pleading with murderous savages, boating down rivers with oars so encrusted with ice as to be barely workable, fish, caught occasionally, freezing to a mass as taken from the net, and having to be "split with a hatchet," the thermometer ranging from 15° to 40° below zero. Staggering with weakness and exhaustion, often half blind, benumbed in limb and dazed in brain, but with never failing pluck, Franklin and his undaunted comrades kept on their way. For this was not a case of leaders only—the rank and file must have their niche of honour for loyal endurance and self-denial. One of the Canadian " Voyageurs," Perrault, presents the officers with a small piece of meat (probably deer or musk ox) saved from his own allowance, " an act," writes Franklin, " at which our eyes were filled with tears." It is pathetic to notice that this good fellow had to fall out and try to get back on their trail. He had been " dizzy," but, after a meal of tea and " some scraps of burnt leather," essayed to plod forward with Sir John and the rest some 200 yards. Then he again became " dizzy," but pushed on for a few minutes, pulled up again, and, bursting into tears, declared he could go no further. He was allowed to turn back towards Dr. Richardson and a temporary halting-place, where the " *tripe de roche* " happened to be plentiful. He never reached there, and is supposed to have been murdered by an Iroquois, one of the traitors of the party. Let our humbler heroes and martyrs have their meed of well-earned fame, and the lasting sympathy of all who love and glory in this " British Empire." Franklin got back to England in 1822, and was not to be satisfied with his enthusiastic reception and the honours conferred upon him. With the persistence of the true

SIR JOHN FRANKLIN.

Britisher, he and his gallant comrades, Richardson and Back, at once volunteered for a further " trip to the North " in 1824. Parry wrote him, as to the narrative, " I need not be ashamed to say that I cried over it like a child. The tears I shed, however, were those of pride and pleasure, pride at being your countryman, brother officer, and friend, pleasure in seeing the virtues of the Christian adding their first and highest charm to the unconquerable perseverance of the officer and the man."

We cannot dwell upon the second expedition, which was to be from the North-American shore, Lake Huron, Superior, Fort William, *en route* to Behring's Straits, and the Mackenzie and Coppermine Rivers, with a view to meet Parry coming westward from Lancaster Sound. Franklin had married in 1823 an accomplished young lady, but their happiness was short-lived, as she died in 1825. Knowing that her days were numbered, she had made for her hero a silk Union Jack, with injunctions as to when and where it was to be hoisted, and even on her death-bed she would not hear of his delaying his departure, but begged him not to halt in his allotted duty merely to close her own eyes. He learnt of her death in New York, and with this stab to his loving nature he went on his way to the silent shores of the frozen North. Of perils and " hair-breadth 'scapes " of every kind there were enough in that second adventure. Weariness, sickness, and strenuous watching were a matter of course, but owing, no doubt, mostly to Franklin's own planning, better provisioning, and the forethought in organisation resulting from previous experience, the thousands of miles surveyed and mapped out in that dreary region were overcome without so many of those ghastly incidents that make the record of the first journey read like the recital of some hideous nightmare. Again he failed to attain the exact objective to which he had devoted himself, but John Franklin's life was the negation of that popular *mot*, "Nothing succeeds like success." Even in his third and fatal attempt he attained only a "*succès d'estime*," but his personality was such that even brilliant success such as the world shouts at could scarcely have added to his fame as martyr to science and national hero. Dr. Richardson wrote of this voyage : "After having served under Captain Franklin for nearly seven years in two successive voyages of discovery, I may be allowed to say . . . that the sentiments of my friends and companions, Captain Back and Lieutenant Kendall, are in unison with my own when I affirm that gratitude and attachment to our late commanding officer will animate our breasts to the latest period of our lives." Still, he had opened up hitherto pathless wastes, and dragged from the reticent Polar mystery a North-American coastline of 1,200 miles. He came home to further honours, received his knighthood in 1829, and the " D.C.L." of Oxford. He married again, and *this*

was the " Lady Franklin " whose faithful love and
pathetic refusal to believe in his death amid those
gloomy solitudes are known to all Englishmen.

Again and again he had attacked the regions of
eternal ice with unfailing pluck and with the simple
confidence of a God-fearing sailor.   Again and
again he returned, with rich results to our knowledge
of the planet on which we live, though not resulting,
as yet, in any practical benefit to Englishmen or
the race in general.   That was not Franklin's
business ; his was " but to do or die," and he did
both.

For a thousand years that " no man's land " of
mystery and peril, which hides the secret of the
North Pole, had magnetised the daring spirits of
Europe.   The very Vikings had pushed their galleys
along its silent shores ; Sebastian Cabot himself
had tried that pathless wilderness ; Frobisher and
Sir Hugh Willoughby, Hudson and Baffin, and a
small host of others, had trodden its white wastes,
and Ross and Parry, McClure, McClintock and Nares
were to follow on.   No matter ! the thing had to
be done, and coy Nature *should* be won over, somehow, by the masterful suitor, Man.   At any rate,
that was the feeling in 1845.

So in the July of that year, having filled in some
gaps in the past years by the Governorship of
Tasmania, and in the Grecian war of liberation,
Franklin sailed with the *Erebus* and *Terror* on that
last fateful voyage.   When asked by official courtesy

whether at sixty he would really like to undertake the job, his reply was " Why, I'm only *fifty-nine !* " Lord Brougham, when told by Herschell of Franklin's appointment, remarked, " Arctic work gets into the blood of these men. They can't help going again if they get a chance ! " He was last spoken with in Baffin's Bay, by a whaler captain in that same month, and then, just fifty-seven years ago, he passed for ever from human sight and the land that loves and honours him. Eleven long years afterwards one of the numerous expeditions sent in search of him by a loving wife and an anxious country came upon the few relics, spared by time and climate, of our gallant knight and his brave crew. Not a man had lived to tell the tale, but a scrap of Government paper recorded that " Sir John Franklin died 11th June, 1847," and that a remnant of the party— never since heard of—were making for the " Great Fish River."

In some unknown grave rests the man who had earned the title of the " greatest explorer " of those Arctic wilds—battles and sieges, storms and ship-wrecks, fights with bears and walruses, tedious imprisonments in the dreary ice packs, and hopeless wanderings over frozen seas, all over. He discovered the North-West Passage — the discovery of the human skeleton so far as Cape Herschell by McClintock seems to show this—but he and his sturdy comrades paid the price. They live in his-tory, and so long as undaunted courage, cheerful

The form text reads:

H. M. S. *Ships Erebus and Terror*

28 of May 184 [ ] Lat. 70° 5' N Long. 98°23' W
Wintered in the Ice in

Having wintered in 1846–7 at Beechey Island
in Lat 74° 43' 28" N Long 91° 39' 15" W after having
ascended Wellington Channel to Lat 77° and returned
by the West side of Cornwallis Island

Sir John Franklin commanding the Expedition
All well

WHOEVER finds this paper is requested to forward it to the Secretary of
the Admiralty, London, *with a note of the time and place at which it was
found*; or, if more convenient, to deliver it for that purpose to the British
Consul at the nearest Port.

QUINCONQUE trouvera ce papier est prié d'y marquer le tems et lieu ou
il l'aura trouvé, et de le faire parvenir au plutot au Secretaire de l'Amirauté
Britannique à Londres.

CUALQUIERA que hallare este Papel, se le suplica de enviarlo al Secretario
del Almirantazgo, en Londrés, con una nota del tiempo y del lugar en
donde se halló.

EEN ieder die dit Papier mogt vinden, wordt hiermede verzogt, om het
zelve, ten spoedigste, te willen zenden aan den Heer Minister van de
Marine der Nederlanden in 's Gravenhage, of wel aan den Secretaris der
Britsche Admiraliteit, te London, en daar by te voegen eene Nota,
inhoudende de tyd en de plaats alwaar dit Papier is gevonden geworden.

FINDEREN af dette Papiir ombedes, naar Leilighed gives, at sende
samme til Admiralitets Secretairen i London, eller nærmeste Embedsmand
i Danmark, Norge, eller Sverrig. Tiden og Stœdit hvor dette er fundet
önskes venskabeligt paategnet.

WER diesen Zettel findet, wird hier-durch ersucht denselben an den
Secretair des Admiralitets in London einzusenden, mit gefälliger angabe
an welchen ort und zu welcher zeit er gefunden worden ist.

...ty consisting of 2 Officers and 6 men
...the Ship on Monday 24th May 1847

The GOVERNMENT PAPER found by the SEARCH PARTY,
WITH OTHER RELICS.

By *Permission of*] [Messrs. JACK, *Edinburgh*

kindliness, and fertile resource are valued in this realm of ours, so long will John Franklin be remembered and his name revered. His monument is in Westminster Abbey amongst the nation's great ones, and a statue of him stands in the Market Place of his native town.

> "Not once nor twice in our fair island story
> The path of duty was the way to glory."

The long, wearing years of uncertainty were ended for Lady Franklin by the finding of the relics. She lived on till 1875, and then, at eighty-three, ended *her* pilgrimage.

Professor Beesley, in his " New Plutarch," says : " For the first half of the 19th century Franklin's name is the central one round which those of all other discoverers cluster. His story is to theirs what the main ' Iliad ' is to its episodes, however brilliant." And his fellow Lincolnshire man, Alfred Tennyson, wrote for the cenotaph in Westminster Abbey :

> " Not here ! The White North has thy bones ; and thou,
> Heroic Sailor-soul,
> Art passing on thine happier voyage now
> Toward no earthly Pole."

CHAPTER XIX.

TUDORS AND STUARTS.

OF the "Boy King," Edward VI., Mary of the
sanguinary affix, and even of the great Elizabeth
herself, there is little to record in direct relation to
our shire.   The two former do not appear to have
favoured it with a visit, and the latter, though
frequently through Stamford on her visits to Lord
Burleigh (see "Worthies") is not specially in
evidence at other places.   In his reign of six years
Edward set his youthful hand to many good works,
such as founding the Bluecoat· School in London,
the Grimsby Free Grammar School, and the Louth
Grammar School, two of these at least being notable
for turning out many distinguished men in the
succeeding centuries.   It was somewhere about
in his reign, too, that the decadence of Boston as a
chief Eastern port became pronounced, and was
said to be owing to silting up and want of improved
access to and appliances at the port, the trade
being driven to other places, probably Grimsby and
Lynn for instance.

The five troubled years of Mary's rule were too

much occupied with Spanish intrigue, risks of war, domestic plots, faction fights between Romanists and Anglicans, and promiscuous incinerating of the particular sectarian " dog " which happened at the moment to be " under," to do much in the way of processions or " progresses." No doubt she realised that Lincolnshire was one of the English counties, and that her august father had had an opinion of it rather more pronounced than that of even the average candid friend.

As to the Virgin Queen, we have said a good deal about her *in re* Lord Burleigh (*ante*, pages 95-105), but there is little record of any intercourse with Lincolnshire people beyond the visits to that statesman already alluded to. In 1565 she was at Stamford, and dined at the " White Friary," founded by Henry III., and afterwards backed up by the bounty of the third Edward. She was several times splendidly entertained by Cecil, twenty young and gallant nobles and gentlemen being retained as her special attendants.

In this reign, too, there happened (1571) great storms and floods in Lincolnshire—one ship was driven from the sea to a considerable distance inland and against a house, both being, no doubt, taken a little aback by such an unexpected *rencontre*. A church was destroyed at the same time. There is a quaint story of that storm : " Between Hummerston and Grimsby eleven sheep, belonging to one Master Specers, were lost, ' whose shepherde

about midday comming to his wife asked his dinner,
and shee being more bold than mannerley say'd he
should have none of hir : then she chaunced to look
toward the marshes where the sheepe were, and
sawe the water breake in so fiercely that the sheepe
would be lost if they were not brought from thence,
say'd that he was not a good shepherde that would
not venture his life for his sheepe, and so he went
straight to drive them from thence ; both he and his
sheepe were drowned, and after the water was gone
he was found dead, standing upright in a ditch.' "

Bourne was overflowed to midway of the height
of the church ! Holbeach, Steeping, Long Sutton,
and other places suffered grievously, and there was
" great losse of cattell " and " many sheepe." It
was of this storm that Jean Ingelow writes in her
poem, " A High Tide on the Coast of Lincolnshire " :

> " Then bankes came down with ruin and rout—
> Then beaten foam flew round about—
> Then all the mighty floods were out—
> So farre, so fast the eygre drave,
> The heart had hardly time to beat,
> Before a shallow seething wave
> Sobbed in the grasses at oure feet ;
> The feet had hardly time to flee
> Before it brake against the knee,
> And all the world was in the sea."

Fourteen years after this, Boston and other places
were subject to the horrors of the plague, of which,
however, there remains little record.

It was in 1580 that Mr. Arthur Hall, M.P. for Grantham, and one of an old Lincolnshire family, got into trouble for publishing a libellous pamphlet accusing his fellows of drunkenness, undue devotion to some heathen deity he called Bacchus, and "other slanderous and derogatory abuse." The Honourable House was, of course, very much scandalised, it being very well known that nobody ever drank too much in those days, and that M.P.'s especially never "indulged," or "hardly ever." The "House" interviewed Mr. Hall at the "bar," and took its change out of him by a fine of 500 marks and expulsion for the remainder of that Parliament. He seems to have refused to retract, and to have taken his punishment "standing."

It may be just worth noting that the Lincolnshire men contemporary with Elizabeth and contributing more or less to the glory of her reign were : Cecil, Lord Treasurer ; Clinton, Lord Admiral ; Anderson, Lord Chief Justice ; Bartie, Lord General in France ; Wilson, Secretary of State ; Heneage, Privy Councillor ; and Whitgift, Archbishop of Canterbury.

The first "progress" of King James I. through his new kingdom was in the spring of 1603, and on the heath (Earpington) approaching Stamford a quaint incident occurred. James noticed a squad of 100 or so giants stalking towards the procession, as the old chronicle says, "like the Patagones, huge long fellowes of twelve and fourteene foote high, that are reported to live on the Mayne of Brazil, neere to the Streights of Megallant. The King at the first sight wondered what they were," but portent and foreboding soon resolved itself into plain prose and common-place in the shape of a party of Fen men on high stilts to present a petition. James rode through the town in great state, having the sword borne before him, " the people joyfull on all parts to see him," and so away again southward. It is doubtless very important to notice that on this occasion " the Alderman and his brethren " attended the King on horseback—Aldermen *could* usually ride in those days.

In the spring of 1617 James (with his Queen, Anne of Denmark) passed through Lincolnshire on a visit to Scotland. He passed a night at Belton (seat of the Pakenham's, Brownlow family), near Grantham, and so on to Lincoln the following morning. There seems to have been the usual fussiness as to reading addresses, deputations, etc., but the King showed unusual good sense in giving it to be understood that " His Highness did not love long speeches." There was much tendering of Sheriffs' staves and the city sword by the Mayor, just within the " Barrgates," and then on to the Minster West Front, where the King kneeled on a cushion and under a canopy, and said prayers, much as Henry VIII. had done, passing into the choir, and " there sate by the Bishop's pue hanged about by rich hangings in a chair all prayer time, Mr.

Dean saying prayers, the Mayor holding up the sword before him all prayer time." After service he inspected the Cathedral, looked round the monuments, saw the Chapter House, and thence passed to his carriage, the Mayor, Aldermen, and Citizens attending him on horseback " to his lodging at St. Catherine's, down Potters-gate Head."

It is cheering to hear that James went to the Cathedral again next morning and healed " fifty persons of the evil." Fifty is a nice even number to pledge oneself to. The old chronicler from whom we quote knew nothing of your new-fangled " agnosticism " and such nonsense, and took his newly-spawned legends boldly and freely, recording them in all good faith. It is singular to notice, however, that James went again the *next* day and cured fifty-three of the same complaint, and that happened to be the 1st of April, 1617.

There was a " great horse race " on the heath, some hunting, a fencing match by the " schollers of the City," cock fighting " at the sign of the George, by the Stanbowe," and other junketings, with which James appears to have made the most of his time. He left next day for Newark.

In 1608 James went through with the Boston Corporation what seems to have been a rather popular form of amusement, viz., he granted another Charter, renewing and confirming the older ones, with fresh privileges and immunities. This sort of thing had been also done by Edward VI., Mary, and

Elizabeth, and Boston wants or Boston " pushful-
ness " must have been kept pretty well to the fore.

But Boston has other claims to lasting fame. It
was from that old-time port that certain of the
Pilgrim Fathers sailed in the *Mayflower* (1602), with
the first seeds of that great Commonwealth now so
keenly rivalling its mother state. Gainsboro' and
Retford men were of that little party, and they
founded the colony of Plymouth. Afterwards, the
Recorder of Boston (Bellingham), and one Leverett
(Alderman), went over; they founded the new
" Boston " over sea, and were accompanied by the
Vicar (Cotton), who had resigned his living on
being " attached " for giving the Sacrament to his
people " sitting ! "   It is of some good augury that
the American Boston assumes, and is mostly acknowledged to be, the very centre of light and
leading in the " States."

And now there looms up from the descending
years the sombre, pathetic figure of the unhappy
Stuart, doomed to a life and death struggle with his
people, and to pay a bitter penalty for venturing
once again to pit " prerogative " against " people."
The midnight screams of the murdered Edward II.
in Pomfret Castle, and the forlorn " finishing " of
Richard II. 'neath Berkeley Towers, raised no such
reverberating echo throughout Europe and the then
known world as the public decapitation of an an-
ointed King in the face of subjects, awestruck at the
audacity of so daring a new departure, and looking on

as at the outpouring of one of the very apocryphal
" vials " itself. Lincolnshire becomes linked with
the history of Charles I. by the fact that in 1626,
the year after his accession, the reclamation of
the large tract known as the " Bedford Level "
was undertaken and successfully carried out by
one Van Vermuyden, a Dutchman, and others
of that country; also, some seven years after,
when he slept a night at St. Martin's, Stamford, on his road to Scotland to be recognised as
King of that country. He again passed through
that town with Queen Henrietta Maria on the
occasion of his visit to the Earl of Westmoreland in
1634. The black clouds of revolution were already
fast gathering, although years were yet to elapse
before the tempest should burst. In 1641 the
plague was about again, some 500 or 600 being
victims in Stamford alone. It was in 1642 that the
town of Boston, with Lynn and other seaports,
was directed to receive a garrison to hold for the
King, to which Parliament responded by drawing a
general order to " oppose that illegal act."

At the beginning of the Civil War Charles
visited Lincoln (July, 1642) and received by
the mouth of Mr. Recorder Dailson professions
of loyalty and support from the Corporation and
people. He called together the " nobility, knights,
gentry and freeholders " of the county, and made
them a speech justifying his course of action and
claiming their allegiance. There is a quaint account

P

of this in the British Museum, superscribed "From Lincolne, July 15th, 1642" : "It was apprehended (by those of quickest insight into publick affairs) that our county (in these distracted Times) was likely to prove the Stage of some dismall Tragedy (the seat of a deplored Warre). Whereupon the prudence and providence of some . . . were awakened to endeavour his Majesties Visit of this County. . . . Four fore Miles the way was a throng, which received our Soveraigne all along with such Peales of shouts and vocall acclamations (A King ! A King ! A King !) as aboundantly testified the Joy, and loyaltie of our Hearts, all our Bodies animated as it were with one Soule, willing, if possible (in a Voice to our dread Soveraigne) to have breathed it out in gratulations. The Gentry (not satisfied with sound) all drew their swords, ready to plead His Majesties Rights with the utmost hazards. The Clergy, computed between two and three hundred, ecchoed out, and redoubled their gratulatory salutations (Vivat Rex !), with such a pleasingnesse and content to His Majestie as He vouchsafed a Princely Recognition of their Dutiful Expression. . . . His Majesty commanded Sir John Monson to Reade to us in His owne Presence an everlasting Witnesse of His gracious Goodnesse, which envy will never staine, nor time perish. . . . The City, pregnant with like joyfull conceptions, was delivered of his congratulations by the Recorder, the proper Organ for those Conveyances, who may well beare a part in this rare Consort, whereto His Majesty *Ex Tempore*, made a gracious answer to every Branch. The whole Corporation awaited with a full Appearance of their Trained Bands and all other possible solemnity they could expresse upon so short a notice. . . . the Prime Gentry of our County presented an humble Petition to His Majesty, by the Hand of the right Honorable the Lord Willoughby of Ersebie, which found a most gracious acceptance, and received a no lesse gracious answer : That for His Person, Crown, Estate, or Postcrity, He neither expected, nor desired their, nor any of His Subjects' assistance, longer than he should protect them, their Religion, Lawes, Interests, and just Rights of Parliament. In which Cases, let the Tongue cleave to the Roofe of that Mouth that speaks, and Hand wither from that Arme, that moves against Him. . . . The last place brings in a List of those many Worthies of our Country, who after the famous example of the Noble Volunteers of Israel, in the dayes of Deborah, offered themselves willingly the Lord's Assistants, by furnishing his Annointed Vicegerent, upon the grounds and for the ends in the Declaration specified, with some Troops of Horses for publique service in the Countrie's safety."

Then in 1643 came an order enforcing " Ship money " from Lincoln, Boston, Spalding, Grimsby, Gainsboro', Wainfleet, and Barton-on-Humber. Most of the strong places were held by the Royalists,

and it is remarked that "two small castles in
Lincolnshire" formed part of the exceptions.
Numbers of the Shire people had been and were
still being indicted at Grantham and other places
for High Treason in siding with the Parliament,
amongst them Sir Anthony Irby and William Ellis,
the two Members for Boston. Grantham was held
by Charles, having been taken by Colonel Cavendish
in March, 1642, with numerous Parliamentary
prisoners, arms, ammunition, etc. It was here,
too, that in the following year Cromwell was on the
scene and defeated with his own regiment twenty-
four troops of the Royalist cavalry. He wrote one
of his "crowning mercy" sort of despatches:
"God hath given us this evening a glorious victory,"
and so on to the finish; "I believe some of our
soldiers did kill two or three men a piece; we have
also gotten some of their officers, and some of their
colours; but what the number of dead is or what
the prisoners, for the present we have not time to
inquire into." After one or two morning calls at
Croyland Abbey, which he honoured by "besieging,"
and Peterboro' Minster, leaving in each case effective
evidence of his passage, he marched on to Stamford.
He seems to have got back to Boston, as for the
rest of that year the town was full of his troops, and
a battle was fought at Winceby, near Horncastle,
variously dated October 6th and 10th, the Royalists
being badly whipped—Oliver slept at Boston the
night before the battle. A good deal of fighting

went on also in and around Gainsboro', the Duke of Newcastle being opposed to Cromwell, and on one occasion beating his troops back to Lincoln, then held by the Parliament. Gainsboro' had to surrender to the Royalists, but in June, 1644, there was a considerable and rather decisive battle, in which General Cavendish was killed and his force routed. Cromwell's despatch says : " About a mile and a half from the town we met the forlorn of the enemy, and drove a troop of their dragoons back upon their main body. We advanced and came to the bottom of a steep hill, which we could not get up but by some tracks, and the body of the enemy endeavoured to hinder us ; but we prevailed, and gained the top of it. A great body of the enemy's horse faced us there, at about a musket shot distance, and a good reserve of a full regiment of horse behind it. . . . General Cavendish charged the Lincolneers and routed them ; immediately I fell on his rear with my three troops, which did so astonish him that he gave over the chase, and would have delivered himself from me. I pressing on, forced him down a hill, and below it, drove the General and some of his soldiers into a quagmire, where my Captain General slew him with a thrust under his short ribs. The rest of the body was totally routed, not one man staying in the place."

This kind of thing, however, was going on all over the country, the Royalists being gradually worsted, so that in 1646, when Charles had to fly

from Oxford in the guise of a serving-man, he slept,
once more, a homeless fugitive, at Stamford.   There
followed the hopeless negotiations, " the chaffering "
and quibbling over a crown and a life, and the
" black and red " tragedy of January 29th in
front of Whitehall.

SOMERSBY RECTORY. (Birthplace of Alfred Tennyson.)

[G.M.P

CHAPTER XX.

ALFRED TENNYSON.

THE reader will sympathise with us in our desire that the order in which we have taken note of our Lincolnshire great ones shall not be confused with our appreciation of the proper place of each on the county scroll of fame. Tennyson may be last in these papers, but he is surely first in the heart of every Lincoln body who can reverence greatness, combined with simplicity of life, strength and brilliancy of intellect, linked with purity and sweetness, and who can bow before a long life, harmonious in purpose and fulfilment and beautiful in its completion, even " from the rising of the sun to the going down thereof."

Strange, that such a spirit should have arisen amongst these wolds and fens of ours ! For, in sooth, the county, though second of the kingdom in size and wealth of natural production, was not the sort of soil to be indicated by " the man in the street " as the birthplace of a great poet. By common repute (so often an egregious liar and scandal-monger) Lincolnshire was not exactly the

generator of soft and mellifluous verse or stirring
and high-toned epic. It was as though the genius
of the county had risen in some wrath, and waving
her star-tipped wand had cried, " You think the
only soul we have is in these potatoes and turnips
and those wide stretches of wheat and barley ;
you think, do you, that we are engrossed in the
best methods of fattening hogs, and that we have
searched after the most effective sheep-wash as for
hid treasure. Behold ! " and Alfred Tennyson
was born.

This was at the old Rectory of Somersby and in
1809, in mid career of meteor-Napoleon and with
the clash of arms all round Europe. Contrast
Jena, Austerlitz, and Leipsic, their thunders and
their slaughter, with the peaceful rustic parsonage,
and a good-looking little English lad trotting about
the garden and paddock with his playmate brother,
within sight of an ancient church, every line of
which seems reminiscent of old-time worship, and
whose walls had for so long echoed to psalm and
anthem, and to such solemn strains as :

> " God of our fathers ! be the God
> Of our succeeding years."

In the veins of that lad ran, through the D'Eyncourts, a considerable tinge of Norman blood
mingled with the merchant-trader element on the
mother's side, and tempered also by such clerical
ancestry and associations as tended to evolve a

gentleman, a scholar, and a man of deep and tender thought upon all the serious problems of life. For a time, like thousands of other immature enthusiasts, he took Byron for his idol, and when that great but ill-disciplined soul broke its tenement of clay at Missolonghi, and fled from the scene of its triumphs, its vagaries, and its disappointments, the boy Tennyson cut on some sandstone rocks at the end of the " glen " at Somersby the words, " Byron is dead," and spoke of the event to his intimates as though a light of the world had been quenched and the future of English poetry was now indeed dark.

As he grew in wisdom and in stature the Byronic afflatus, if it is to be so called, passed from his spirit like some sickly vapour, and the boyish worship of gloomy cynicism or reckless Bohemianism gave place to a more refined, cultured, and spiritual interpretation of things, expressed withal in manly and vigorous measures. He had been sent as a boy of seven to Louth Grammar School, following in the track of Sir John Franklin, and we may here mention that which " grapples him " to our Lincolnshire hearts still tighter with " hooks of steel," viz., that when later on he took to himself his life's partner, it was in the person of a niece of that gallant sailor and explorer.

But of his school days there is no extravagantly pleasant record. There was a wayward-tempered thrashing master of the old school, and it would seem that life there and at that time could not have

been *very* much worth living. One can faintly
imagine the feelings of a delicate, sensitive-minded
lad like Tennyson, as he sat on the school steps one
cold winter's morning " crying bitterly," poor mite ;
after being soundly cuffed, in the then accepted
fashion, by one of the school bullies for having committed the unpardonable offence of being a " new
boy." But this childish trouble passed, and, eleven
years old, the young Alfred was recalled home to
work with his father. It is rather a touching
incident that, nearly fifty years later, the great
poet sent his old master a copy of his own complete
works, and the old pedagogue replied (then in his
eighty-sixth year) in a tone of quaint scholastic
pedantry, and with a not too gushing appreciation—
Louth School had " entertained angels unawares."

His earliest holidays as a boy were often with
his father and mother and the other boys at Mable-
thorpe, and long years after he loved to return to
look on the North Sea, with its :

" . . . hollow ocean ridges, roaring into cataracts,"

and over the flats at eventide, and

" . . . the wide-winged sunset of the misty marsh."

After the first one or two volumes of youthful
verse by the brothers Alfred and Charles, in which
the former was just preening his wings for higher
flights, came at last " In Memoriam," the noblest
epitaph ever written for man. It was a notable

instance of one gracious and beautiful life absorbed
into and " informing " another and yet higher
career.   In this outburst of a stricken and bereaved
soul the poet voices the vague unrest then creeping
over, and now almost enveloping, the latter-day
spirit of enquiry and of desire after we know not
what.   The pathetic doubt, the earnest questioning
which would merge into faith if it only could, and
the almost despairing cry, are all here :

> " Behold we know not anything,
>
> .   .   .   .
>
> As children crying in the night,
> And with no language but a cry."

This is not a biography, but rather an appreciation.   Need we presume to instruct Lincolnshire folk as to their own poet ?   Who, of any kind
of culture or thought, has not read the " Idylls,"
" Maud,"   " Enoch Arden,"   " The Holy Grail,"
" The Lovers' Tale," " Locksley Hall," " The Cup
and Falcon," " Queen Mary," " Harold," " Becket,"
and the rest ?   They form a wondrous " tale of
work " even for a life ending at eighty, in that moon-
lit chamber, with the upturned massive face resting
in its own white, kingly calm.   And for those who
had little of " thought " for letters or poetic force,
and less of " culture "—well ! we can quote the
story told in the " Life," by the present Lord
Tennyson.   A Yorkshire man, with a talent for
recitation, was staying at a farmhouse in Holderness,

where neighbours used to look in for a smoke and a chat. He gave them, no doubt in good Lincolnshire form, the " Northern Farmer." One of the company cried, " Dang it ! that caps owt. Now, sir, is that i' print ? If it be I'll buy t'book, cost what it may." The guest replied, " The book has things you mayn't like so well. I'll write it out for you." He did so, and the farmer put the paper in his breast pocket. Next day when out shooting with others of the party he was seen from time to time to take it out and read it. We mustn't say this was Beauty charming the Beast. We can adopt the biographer's more elegant simile of Orpheus calling around him such of animated nature as might be at all teachable.

He was full of rugged stories, racy of the soil and dialect. We can give but two: those who want more must go to the enthralling " Life " by the Poet's eldest son. A farmer, talking over the Sunday sermon in which the endless fires of hell had been picturesquely worked in : " Noa, Sally ! It we'ant do. Noa constitution could stan' it " ; and a parson's prayer for rain, " Especially on John Stubbs' field in the middle marsh, and, if thou doest not know it, it has a big thorn tree in t' middle o't." Well might a farmer's daughter, as is related, exclaim, on hearing some of these things " Why ! that's labourers' talk. I thought Mr. Tennyson was a gentleman ! "

We may just note, however, that the happy quiet

TENNYSON.

From the Photo by]

[BARRAUDS, *London*

and joyful intercourse with kindred spirits at
Haslemere and Freshwater, with all that it produced
for us, did not obliterate the vivid sense of the poet
for what some people hold to be the doubtful beauties
of his native county and its coast.

" Calm and deep peace on these high wolds."

" The crowded farms and lessening towers."

" The water curled,
The cattle huddled on the lea,
And, wildly dashed on tower and tree,
The sunbeam strikes along the world."

" The drain cut levels on the marshy lea,
Grey sandbanks and pale sunsets, dreary wind,
Dim shores, dense rains, and heavy clouded sea."

" The thicket stirs,
The fountain pulses high in sunnier jets,
The blackcap warbles and the turtle purrs,
The starling claps its tiny castanets."

These were the sort of lines, threaded together
like silver beads, that resulted from Tennyson's
wanderings over breezy upland, monotonous fen,
and the rather " sad sea waves " of our prosaic
shire.

But the inner spirit of all he wrote ! The human
weakness of the Grand Knight Lancelot, the failure
of Guinivere, the pure and gallant Sir Galahad,
Merlin the Sage, Vivien the Enchantress, and the
whole gallery of " warriors true and ladies fair,"

with the all but divine Arthur towering above them in misty isolation, the pathetic patience and martyr-like resignation of the homely Enoch, and the half hidden suggestion to virtue and manliness (when face to face with the choice between good and evil) which glistens like a golden thread through all his verse, stamp Alfred Tennyson as the interpreter of his age, its weariness alike of creeds and cant and cynics, its longing after a brighter and purer future, and its half-formed resolution to quit the whole senseless muddle of cheating trade, murderous competition, squalid poverty, and pinchbeck ambitions, for the straight and narrow path of wholesome living and a " fair chance for all." He was pin-pricked, of course, by some of the literary rowdies who pose as critics. He was soft, forsooth ! effeminate ! namby-pamby, wanted " backbone," meaning that he was not sufficiently fleshly, and had not enough about him of that transcendent beauty, the " man of the world." From the sneer as to want of virility he stands acquitted by such poems as " The Revenge," " The Charge of the Light Brigade," and that trumpet-call, " Riflemen ! Form ! " which rang through our land some fifty years ago, and which was one of the direct agencies resulting in our present day half million volunteers for the defence of the country.

Long after the " man of the world " has gone to his own place, and when all the cynics are snapping and snarling at each other below, the thoughts and

words of Alfred Tennyson will be inspiring and
guiding the best and highest of our race and
shaping the future of mankind.

> " Hold thou the good, define it well,
>   For fear divine philosophy
>   Should push beyond her mark and be
>   Procuress to the Lords of Hell."

Away in the far Arctic North, Dr. Kane and his
comrades, in one of the Grinnell expeditions, looking
out over the dreary waste, and thinking of the gentle
melancholy of some of his descriptions, and especially
no doubt, of the epitaph to Franklin, already quoted,
named after him a natural rock column, 480 feet
high, and there amid the eternal silence, akin surely
to Carlyle's " immensities," stands " Tennyson's
Monument," its towering crag not more endurable
than his own world-wide fame.

CHAPTER XXI.

UNTO THESE LAST.

FROM this time on there are few Royal visits or matters of historical importance to dwell upon. Cromwell, after his fighting power gave place to the still more wearing cares of statesman and practical Monarch, had little time for local detail. It may, however, be here mentioned that in his sketch of Cromwell, which Mr. John Morley has published, he mentions this incident : Lord Exeter came to Major-General Whalley, Oliver's head man for the district, to know if, *pace* the efforts of the Puritans to stop all sports, he would allow the Lady Grantham Cup to be run for at Lincoln, as, if so, he would start a horse ; and Whalley reported to the Protector, " I assured him that it was not your Highness' intention, in the suppression of horse races, to abridge gentlemen of that sport, but to prevent the great confluence of irreconcilable enemies." Lord Exeter ran his horse, but we are not told whether he won or not. Charles II. was too busy with providing us, through his Nell Gwynnes, his Castlemaines, and his Louise de Keroualles, with a considerable section of our modern peerage, to say nothing of his spaniels, the daily urgency of feeding the swans in the park, the " harmless, necessary " walk in the Mall, and keeping well in form for his refreshing " chaffs " with Rochester, Villiers, and Co. One of the few things recorded is that on his accession he managed to find fault with the Mayor and Corporation of Boston, and removed them from office. It looks rather like a spiteful rejoinder to their former prompt protest against " Ship money " and other vagaries of the " Crown." He also renewed the Stamford Charter, and for the first time blessed that ancient town with a Mayor.

It was on Charles' marriage to Catherine of Braganza that, after many vicissitudes, changes of ownership, etc., Spalding Manor became part of her jointure, and remains Crown property to this day.

William III. came through the Shire in October, 1695, and had a great reception in Lincoln. Arrived 7 p.m., no doubt dark. " Torches, links, and flamboys." A kneeling Mayor, the great sword offered, " trumpets, hautboys, and drums—a great company of the body of the city with a great company of gentlemen and others, all on horseback." Speech by the Recorder and the usual innocent formalities, even to dangerous equitation on the part of the said Recorder, the Mayor, and others. William left next day for Welbeck, then the Duke of Newcastle's place.

A prominent man in the second half of the 17th

Q

century was Simon Patrick, a learned writer and powerful controversialist as against some of the Papistical tendencies of his time, born at Gainsboro', 1626. He became Prebendary of Westminster and Dean of Peterboro', taking a leading part in stiffening James II. against his own wobbling towards Rome. He was called on at the Revolution to preach before the Prince and Princess of Orange, became Bishop of Chichester, and afterwards Ely, dying in that town in the ripeness of fourscore, " An honour to the Church and the age in which he lived." He had declined certain diplomatic advances of James with the remark that he " could not give up a religion so well proved as that of the Protestant."

Heavy floods and violent storms continued to afflict the county at intervals, notably 1763-1807, and others, but on the whole the records are meagre. Probably, after many hard knocks in civil commotion, rebellions and foreign wars, our shire began to realise that it was time its " wild oats " were sown and done with. Anyhow, the sentiments of Tennyson's " Lincolnshire Farmer " began to find practical expression in " stubbin' waästes," " plowin' Thurnaby hoalms," and generally " doin' duty by the lond." The size and weight up to which to breed a pig, the amount of wool to be got off a sheep, with the quality of the mutton thereof, and the precise quantity of nutrimental beef to be raised by any conscientious ox, placed by a beneficent providence (and a keen-eyed farmer) upon some of the finest grazing land in the world, henceforth absorbed the main energies of the district, and, as a corollary, there slowly worked out as from day-dream to every-day life a vision of mechanics tendering to man *their* aid in dragging from the land the very utmost it had to give. So Lincoln, Boston, Gainsboro', Grantham, and Stamford have turned out portable engines, steam ploughs, thrashing machines, reapers, elevators, and the rest, not only for the county, but for other of the home lands and foreign and Colonial farms to the four corners of this gyrating planet.

There were curious survivals, however, in spite of all nineteenth century progress. Here is a curious statement from the Rev. Baring Gould's recent book, "In a Quiet Village" (article, "Folk Prayers"). The Vicar of Upton Grey, Winchfield, writes Mr. Gould that he himself had met in the marshes with the following strange survival as a cure for ague. In the autumn of 1857 or 1858 he had taken some quinine to a lad who lived with an old grandmother. On his next visit the old dame scornfully refused to have any more of it, saying she "knowed on a sight better cure nor youn mucky stuff." With that she showed at the bottom of the bed three horseshoes with a hammer cross-wise upon them. On the Vicar showing in-credulity she said, "Na'ay lad, it's a charm. I tak's t'mell (hammer) i' my left ha'an and I mash'ys (strikes) they shoon throice and oi sez:

" Fether, Son, and Holi Ghoast,
   Na'ale the divil to this poast,
   Throice I stroikes with holi crook
   Wun for God and wun fur Wod and wun for Sok."

The clergyman concludes, and Mr. Baring Gould seems to tacitly acquiesce, " Wod " is of course Woden, and " Sok " is the evil god Soki, of Scandinavian mythology.

In 1685 the " Lincolnshire Regiment " first took definite shape, and has a notable history as the, at present, 10th Regiment of foot. James the Second was under pressure from the Duke of Monmouth's rebellion in the West Country, and had to call out forces for its suppression. Our so-called county Regiment was part of these. It sounds quaintly to read of a uniform of blue coat, big sombrero cavalier-like hats, and crimson stockings and knickers, the latter quite baggy and unabashed, apparently with no thought of being taken for either trousers or short hose. Since its formation this gallant corps has seen service in all parts of the world, and has well maintained the reputation of the county. It began by declaring for the Prince of Orange as against James, and so adding to the rolling snowball of forces which finally landed William in London as Monarch of these Islands. It took a critical part in the Battle of Steenkirk against the French (1692), and came out of its baptism of fire, this being its first serious engagement, under the applause of our allies. It took its share of campaigning up to the peace of Ryswick, marching and counter-marching, storming fortified places, crossing rivers in flood, and varied these with garrison duty in English counties and in Ireland. It took part in the siege and capture of Huy, under Marlborough, and the storming of the heights of Schellenberg (1703-4). Then came the great day of Blenheim, when, side by side with the Scots Fusiliers, the 10th attacked the village of that name, but which was too strongly held by a much more numerous body of French. The great victory, however, was won, but cost the Regiment four officers killed, nine wounded, and many of the men, number not reported. Ramilies (1706) followed, where, though late in the day, the 10th was used by Marlborough, with some other corps, to administer the *coup de grace* to the French, and thus score yet another " glorious victory." Their colonel, the gallant Lord North and Grey, was promoted Brigadier-General, and given three battalions of infantry. At Oudenarde and Tournay the Regiment was present, and at Malplaquet, where the loss of officers and men is said to have been greater than at Blenheim, Ramilies, and Oudenarde put together, the Lincolnshire men formed part of a column for storming some formidable and heavily-manned intrenchments in the wood of Taisniere, the Foot Guards leading. The victory (1709) was complete, and we brought off " many prisoners, colours, standards, and cannon." No doubt the remark of the writer who records these things, " the carnage was dreadful," was amply justified. Garrison duty in England again followed ; and then the scene changes indeed, for the 10th were at the first skirmish in the American War of Independence, Lexington (1775), and it is gravely stated that it was by the wounding of a soldier of this Regiment that the first blood was shed in that unhappy contest. At Bunker's Hill the corps was again " to the front," when the English troops gained a victory over a force two or three times as numerous and strongly intrenched. At Long Island, Rhode Island, in New Jersey, and at many other places, in minor battles and skirmishes, the Regiment held its own as strong and sturdy, gallant in attack, dogged and dauntless in defence. A spell of service in India, and afterwards Egypt, without any notable event, followed, but the 10th, in common with the other troops of the expedition against Napoleon, received the Royal permission to bear the " Sphynx " and the word " Egypt " on their colours. The Regiment was sent to back up the Neapolitan Bourbon against Napoleon and his puppet monarch, Murat, and took part in a number of petty fights with the French in Naples and Sicily, then joining the British forces in Spain, with a similar experience, and again returning to Sicily. Since then the corps has done duty at Malta, in the Ionian Islands, Ireland, Portugal, and India, its colours being in the very van at the great battle of Sobraon, where, after

Moodkee, Ferozeshah, and Aliwal, the Sikh power was finally smashed. The 10th formed part of the column ordered to head the attack on the enemy's right, to draw out the fierceness of his defence, and as the Commander-in-Chief (afterwards Lord Gough) put it, to " take off the rough edge of the Sikhs." Lieutenant-Colonel Franks commanding, the 10th advanced over the flat against a hail of fire, and *fired no shot* until within the Sikh intrenchments. The thunder of the most powerful artillery opposed to us by any Indian force, and a tremendous fire from our own guns, gave place to a determined hand-to-hand conflict, but the British had " come to stay," and they have " been there " ever since. It was one of the fiercest battles of modern times, and the Sikh power, represented by 30,000 of the flower of their troops, were practically hurled into and across the Sutlej. The " Lincolnshire " were authorised by Queen Victoria to add " Sobraon " to their colours, and their Colonel got a well-earned " C.B."

In addition to the inscriptions already named, the 10th bears on its colours Blenheim, Ramilies, Oudenarde, Malplaquet, Peninsula, Mooltan, Goojerat, Lucknow (Indian Mutiny), Atbara, and Khartoum, and was also `at Paardeberg and other engagements in the recent South African war.

About 70% of the men are Lincolnshire men, and the county has also its Yeomanry and Militia, in addition to two full active-service companies of Volunteers who went out to the Cape.

Of course, these more modern exploits of the Lincolnshire Regiment synchronised with the reign of her late most gracious and womanly Majesty, Queen Victoria. And here we may mention that more than fifty years ago (1851) that sovereign lady passed through Lincolnshire on her way to Grimsby (to inspect the new docks there) and her well-beloved Scotland. Accompanied by Albert, Prince Consort, the then Prince of Wales, a delicate-looking boy of ten, and the Princess Royal, after-wards Empress of Germany, the Queen arrived at 5.30 p.m. by special Great Northern train, and was received by the Mayor (Mr. Charles Ward) and Corporation, the Sheriff of the County (Sir Charles Anderson), the Town Clerk, Magistrates, Coroner, etc., etc. The Royal Standard floated proudly from the broad tower of the Cathedral, bells were clanging merrily, bands were discoursing sweet music, the whole population of the town and of the districts around was astir, triumphal arches made the venerable City look as though it were renewing its youth, and exuberant loyalty blossomed out in innumerable gaieties of decoration. Of course, the usual and orthodox " address " had to be endured, and, equally of course, was responded to in a " gracious answer," and then, after only sufficient time to comfortably change engines, away sped the train northwards. Lord John Russell (the

" little Lord John " of those days, and to whose
notable career but scant justice is done in our time)
was the Minister in attendance, and some of the
Great Northern directors (of whom Mr. Thomas
Wetherell, a leading Lincoln man, was at that time
one) went forward on the train.   It was a brief
glimpse of the Sovereign, and, so far as we have been
able to ascertain, the only one for some scores of
years, but the County has had a certain amount
of " innings " since in the frequent passage to and
fro of the Prince of Wales, now King Edward, in
his steady patronage of Lincoln races.

Meanwhile, as the Star of Empire, for Britain,
rose steadily to its 20th century zenith, by means
of hardy statesmanship and military prowess, a
brilliant development of national genius went on,
side by side with the thunder of cannon, the popular
shouts for victory, and the sealing, with quiet
assurance, of advantageous treaties.   In the State,
Walpole and George Saville (Marquis of Halifax),
Harley and Bolingbroke, led up to Chatham and
the younger Pitt, to Fox and Grattan, to Edmund
Burke and Canning, to Peel and Gladstone, Beaconsfield and Salisbury.   In arms, a Wellington was
to arise, who should beat back the erstwhile Dictator
of Europe ; Wolfe was to win Quebec, Sir John
Moore was to die at Corunna, and the " Nae-peers "
were to show that the rising realm of the stolid
and sturdy West lacked nothing of elastic vigour in
dealing with the fierce chieftains of the East.   On

the sea, Jervis and Howe, Collingwood and the
idolised Nelson, swept the ocean for its coming
mistress, and held aloft the flag which, sometimes
lowered in untoward misfortune, was never shamed,
and finally floated unquestioned over the " seven
seas." Indomitable travellers explored the wilds
of Australia, of Canada, of Thibet, and the Arctic
regions, and the dark, mysterious and blood-stained
continent of the children of Ham was opened up by
Mungo Park and Robert Moffatt, David Living-
stone and Henry Stanley. The school of English
painting, from Thomas Lawrence and Joshua Rey-
nolds to Leighton and Millais, Holman Hunt and
Alma Tadema, needs not, " with bated breath and
whispering humbleness," deprecate comparisons
with that of other nations high in repute for the
development of art. The music of Calcott and
Purcell, to say nothing of the half-Anglicised
Handel, has gathered from other schools a certain
sweetness as well as lightness of touch, until it comes
before us with the " Golden Legend " and the operatic
daintiness of Arthur Sullivan, and the resonant
harmonies of Stainer, Mackenzie, Goss, Elgar, and
a small host of worthy competitors, the climax
being an English *lady* stepping into the arena and
competing with the mere musical *man* by one of the
most successful and artistically well-applauded
operas of the day. For science, let Newton and
James Watt, Brunel and the Stephensons, Huxley
and Tyndall, Faraday, Darwin, and Lister, speak ;

while, in their several spheres of literature, what an illustrious line we have in Hume, Gibbon, Hallam, and Macaulay, Dr. Johnson, and De Foe ; from Dean Swift to Sheridan, from Addison and Steele to Walter Scott, Dickens and Thackeray. All this is like catalogue-making, but can we omit the opulent and beautiful English of the art master, John Ruskin, the skill and daring of Robert Clive in the far Orient, and the passionate oratory and world-wide influence of Wesley and Whitefield, the masterful word-power of Charles Spurgeon, the more solid, but not more sweeping, rhetoric of Robertson, of Brighton, and the array of great Churchmen of all shades of opinion, whose genius and mighty labours have held up the banner of that " righteousness " which " exalteth a nation " ? And poetry has not lagged behind her sister arts, or the " muse of history," or the keen and restless pursuit of science—Dryden and Pope, the pensive Cowper and the moody Byron, Wordsworth and Shelley, Campbell and Moore and Robert Burns have " passed," but we are yet under the spell of the rugged strength and graphic force of Browning, and the chaste and silvery verse of our own Lincoln-shire-born Tennyson. This brings us to the point that, whether in the " spacious times of great Elizabeth," the almost equally glorious days of Anne and some of the Georges, or these latter-day " Victorian " marvels, the " County " has borne *its* honourable share in British progress, whether in art or science, statesmanship or arms.* She has from time to time added, it is said, by reclamation from the sea and drainage of Fen land, some thousand square miles of cultivable soil to her former area.† May she, in far greater ratio, go on in mental, moral, and artistic advancement until she makes dim the honourable record of the past in the still brighter glories of the future !

* A Lincolnshire man, Robert Manning, of Bourne, gave much of its present shape to the English language.

† The wonderful tenacity and vigorous spreading power of the little " Marram," and other plants, holding the sand and silt, catching up tiny deposits of sea waste, and gradually forming a bank over which the " mighty monster " can no longer wash as he pleases, is one of the most curious of studies. The work has gone on notably in Skegness and the neighbourhood. It is credibly stated that the little shoots multiply 500-fold in a single year. The " warp " land, too, all around Crowle and the district gives forth year by year its smiling harvests, where formerly the coasting trader steered his rude craft or the Viking sailed in all the panoply of war (see *Windsor Magazine*, August, 1902).

WARD, LOCK & CO., LIMITED, LONDON, NEW YORK, AND MELBOURNE.

22